Watermelon Pie
and Other Slices!

Interactive Songs, Poems, Charts, and Games

PreK through 2nd Grade

By Sharon MacDonald

Grasshopper Press
15215 Chalet Drive
San Antonio, Texas

This book is dedicated to my husband, George. Without his support, suggestions, encouragement...and peeks, from time to time, this book would not have happened.

I dedicate it also to my three children, Brad, Meg, and John Douglas. They listened to my songs every morning, instead of their alarm clocks. Captives to the end, they endured. And, in later years they recalled as adults that they loved them.

Editor: G. T. Nave
Illustrator: Sharon MacDonald

Entire contents Copyright © 2000 Grasshopper Press. However, the individual purchaser of this book may reproduce designated materials for the classroom and for individual use. The purchase of this book does not entitle reproduction of any part for an entire school, a district, or a school system. Such use is strictly prohibited.

ISBN 0-9705949-1-7

Some Words About Teachers, Young Children and Songs

Teachers of young children are up against an immovable wall of time. There just isn't enough time to get ready each day—to teach, to review and then, to assess the children's progress (it is hard to find time for a potty break, too!).

Because of the limited time, I try to teach several subjects at the same time. When I am doing morning group, for example, I add math and reading and I share the pen with the children in the group who are ready to write. Using a center-based classroom I blend the essential curriculum skills and concepts into each center so that wherever a child works she is learning to read and to do math while working with science, fine arts, and writing activities. Songs need to teach, as well. As I said, there is so little time and so much to do.

Over the years I read a few research studies on the advantages of using music in the classroom. Findings have been generally inconclusive. Music has been shown to help with discipline. There has been little research, however, about how songs, chants, and lullabies influence learning. There are valid conclusions and extensions one can make about how well songs work, however. History tells us....

For thousands of years, people have sung for enjoyment and to ease the burdens of work. Music and songs have conveyed important information about one's family and culture. This is true for all cultures across the world. Songs, poems, chants, and rhymes, for example, made it possible for workman in the Middle Ages to be organized to build great cathedrals. They could not learn through reading and writing since few could do either. Recent research on the effects of music on the brain concludes that the brain loves music and that facts traveling on musical notes are learned more quickly, and better retained for speedy, accurate retrieval. The research certainly corroborates my 28 years of teaching. There are many reasons for children to sing!

When I choose songs well I can teach reading, writing, math, science, fine arts, social studies, language, and motor skills. The results are striking, especially with children with special needs and those who have had problems in more structured settings.

Choosing the right songs matters. There are lots of choices today. Some are fun to sing and useful; others are not well suited for teaching young children. Let's look at one: *Rock A Bye Baby*.

> *Rock a bye baby in the treetop*
> *When the wind blows the cradle will rock*
> *When the bough breaks, the cradle will fall*
> *And down will come baby, cradle and all.*

What does it teach? Here is an interpretation:

> Babies may be put in cradles and hanged in tree branches (called "boughs"). This is done to free up mother's hands so she can do other things, like work hard. Wind may blow the baby around and cool her but she will fall to the ground when the tree branch breaks.

What did we learn? It was written and sung during the Colonial Period. It accurately described everyday life back then. Things have changed. *Rock a Bye Baby* is not quite the right song. It is out of date. So.... What <u>are</u> we looking for in a song?

Let's lot at the elements of songs that teach (please note that you are <u>not</u> going to find every element discussed below in a song you choose):

<u>*They are relevant, meaningful and interesting to the children.*</u>
Use songs that peak children's interest. Turn their interest into opportunities to teach. Teach through song rather than drill.

<u>*They tell a simple story.*</u>
Use songs that have a beginning, middle, and an end so that children develop an understanding of "storyness." Some good examples in this book are *The Crayon Box*, *Painting*, and *How Do You Do?*

They have a simple, memorable melody. If you hear your children humming or singing the song on the playground, you have a winner. Use the song to build skills.

They build a base for future learning. Often we are asked to teach information that the children are not ready to learn or to teach a skill that is beyond their levels of ability. When this happens, select a song that has some of the information in it that you need to teach. The children will learn it and be able to recall it months later when it will mean something to them.

They review information and practice skills.
Look at the skills and concepts you taught during the year. To review, teach a song that contains some of the information you have taught. Let the singing of the song help re-teach and review for the children what they have learned. Let's assume, for example, that you are teaching the color words like red, green, and yellow. Use the song *Crayons (in this book)* with an interactive chart; use the activities described. All of the activities will give the children many opportunities to practice the color words.

They are age appropriate. Sing wisely. *Throw Mama Off The Train* is not age appropriate!

Using songs to teach saves the teacher's time. Songs help young children learn information quickly and accurately. Songs help children store and retrieve information longer.

Sing!

Just a Note: I suggest that you use "just for fun" songs, too. But, be aware of the limitations of the songs you sing. My children loved Shel Silverstein's poem *I'm Being Swallowed by a Boa Constrictor*. It was adapted to song. We sang it just for fun! The children learned about body parts and I think it introduce them to their emerging sense of humor. They added two new words to their vocabulary, too: *boa constrictor*.

Table of Contents

Introduction		1
1	Watermelon Pie	12
2	The Crayon Box	14
3	Zip Up Your Jacket	17
4	Peanut Brown	19
5	Little Tree House	24
6	Sing a Song of Apples	26
7	Painting	31
8	Up and Down	37
9	Here is a Bunny	39
10	Crayons	43
11	Six Little Frogs	48
12	Leaves	54
13	Ish Biddley Otten Dotten	58
14	Brown, Round Tree	59
15	Cup Tapping	69
16	Name Game	74
17	How Do You Do?	76
18	Jump Down Turn Around	78
19	Pepperoni Pizza	80

What is Interactive Learning?

Interactive learning is what happens when a child is involved directly in an activity, learning by doing. It is a two-way process: The child acts on the activity; the activity elicits a response from the child. The child has choices to make. The interaction adds to the child's storehouse of knowledge. In the interactive model, children are active participants, not spectators.

The activities in this book have been designed to get the children involved. They teach the skills and concepts young children need to learn. Most of the activities can be self-directed. Some examples of self-directed activities are oral and written language exercises that ask the children to find words and letters, or to fill-in a word in a line of poetry.

Interactive learning is best achieved by using multiple-sensory channels--like seeing, hearing, touching, smelling, tasting, and singing. Information stored in this way is more easily retained and retrieved later. If children can hear, touch, sing, and read a word, for example, they learn it; and they will retain it for a long time. Let's look at learning the word *rough*, for example. If a child *felt* sandpaper, as well as *listened to, read,* and *sang* the word rough, the child would know what rough meant; it would be unlikely that he would ever forget it. Using two sensory channels to impart information is good; using three is optimum. It is not such a hard thing to add a component to an activity you are doing already to make it interactive. For example, you can match words, highlight letters, or add physical movement to any learning experience.

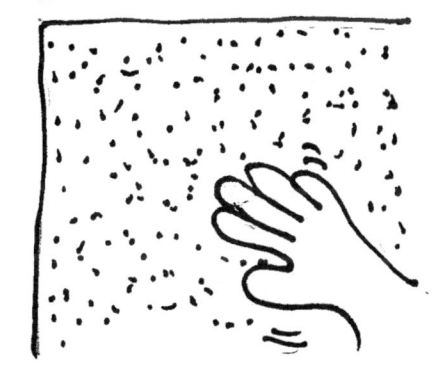

The Children Do Something With the Materials

Interactive means that the children *do something* with the materials. It means they help write stories and share them; record "research" results; move around puzzle pieces, and feel the texture of objects. *Interactive* work is a constructive, positive process, taking place in a structured setting. It is not in itself noisy or confusing. In summary, children gather information more easily, and they retain more completely, when they:

>   Touch, feel, and fiddle with things,
>   Move things around using their hands, feet, and bodies,
>   Sing, chant, listen, and repeat words and phrases; and,
>   Twist, stir, taste, and smell.

Reading skills can be taught interactively, also. Since learning to read is among the most important goals of early education, teaching reading interactively broadens the reading experience for the child. There are other skills, too, like math, writing, listening, spelling, and oral language that can be taught using interactive methods. We will have more on that later.

Let's look at an example of the effectiveness of interactive learning from our collective pasts. Remember *Mickey Mouse*? Can you spell it? Spell it. How did you do it? Sing it? Sure. Because you learned it as a song, and sung it often, *Mickey* is much easier to spell than, say, *Donald Duck*? What a powerful way it was to learn to spell.

The interactive possibilities of writing are different. Writing itself is *interaction*. What is missing for the child is a *reason* to write. Here is a list of the ways you can give the children a reason to write.

> ➢ Make a grocery list
> ➢ Share the pen among the children during morning message

- Add something to the "Must Do" class list
- Write a note to a friend
- Document their "scientific" research
- Label block constructions
- Create a menu
- Write a class thank you note
- Make signs
- Write a story to share with others
- Write down pretend phone messages
- Write important events on a calendar
- Tell how to make a peanut butter and jelly sandwich
- Describe their drawings and pictures
- Make a big book
- Write a get well card to a relative or friend
- Write on your "Remember to Bring it to School" list
- Write pumpkin words on a pumpkin with a *Visa Visa*

The battle for you will be in getting the children excited about writing; half the battle is won if they write about things that are important to them.

We have talked about using interactive activities to teach reading. We can use them to help teach math, as well. The following poem and activity are examples of math, but they still have the reading and listening components. The activity shows you how to make this poem interactive, or any other poem you select. If you do several things to the same poem, song, or story, you will cut down the number of interactive charts you need to make.

Five Round Pumpkins*
By Sharon MacDonald

Five round pumpkins
In a road side store
One became a jack-o-lantern
And then there were four.

Four round pumpkins
As orange as can be
One became a pumpkin pie
Then there were three.

Three round pumpkins
With nothing fun to do
One was cooked as pumpkin bread
And then there were two.

Two round pumpkins
Basking in the sun
One was cooked as pancakes
Then there was one.
One round pumpkin
One job was left undone
So he was kept to make new seeds
And then there were none.

*From <u>Everyday Discoveries: Amazingly Easy Science and Math Activities Using Stuff you Already Have</u> by Sharon MacDonald, published by Gryphon House.

Put the poem on a chart with a piece of soft-side Velcro placed below each number word. Write the number words and the numbers "1," "2," "3," "4," and "5" on short sentence strips. Put a small piece of hook-side *Velcro* (or sandpaper) on the back of the numbers and the number words. Have the children put either the number word, or number itself, below each number word. Please see Activity 7 for more ideas.

<u>Interactive learning gives us a way to:</u>

- Attract children to print
- Make work *relevant to the children's experiences*
- Allow children to work at their own ability level
- Help the children see themselves as readers
- Have the children review the skills they have learned
- Encourage the children to practice what they have learned
- Learn to problem-solve other ways of working with materials
- Work independently
- Assume more responsibility for some aspects of their own learning
- Assess the learning taking place continuously
- Build self-confidence
- Teach children how to be a tutor
- Develop higher level thinking skills
- Work cooperatively with others
- *Use poems, songs, chants, jingles, and sayings to invite the children to participate*

Children need to acquire specific skills to be successful readers. The skills are listed below. Activities to build these skills need to be repeated over-and-over again. Repetition builds skills. Using interactive games, materials, and equipment, makes repetition fun; and creates new avenues to successfully re-teach and review previously learned skills.

(Note: The skills list below focuses on literacy only; other curriculum areas would invite a list of different skills. Most curriculum concepts can be taught interactively, using many of the ideas presented in this book.)

Literacy Skills Learned Through Interactive Activities

- ✓ Directionality
- ✓ Letter recognition
- ✓ Rhyming words
- ✓ Root words
- ✓ Vowel sounds
- ✓ Beginning- and ending sounds
- ✓ Beginning
- ✓ Ending blends
- ✓ Punctuation
- ✓ Spacing
- ✓ CVC
- ✓ CVCE
- ✓ Differences between letters and words
- ✓ One-to-one correspondence
- ✓ Letter formation
- ✓ Onset and rime
- ✓ Prefix and suffix
- ✓ Diagraphs
- ✓ Diphthongs
- ✓ Contractions
- ✓ Syllabication
- ✓ Vowel patterns
- ✓ Alliteration

How to Make Activities Interactive

There are many ways to make interactive materials; take a skill or a concept you want to teach and put it,

in:

A book of movable parts
A folder game
A pocket chart
Resealable bags
A pizza box or shoebox
Baskets, buckets, tote trays

on:

Charts and posters
An old game board
An overhead
A magnet- or flannel board
A bulletin board
A dry-erase marker on board
Pizza circle

To make the pieces moveable use:

- ✓ Velcro
- ✓ Brads
- ✓ Sticky Tac
- ✓ Magnetic strips
- ✓ Vinyl covers
- ✓ Removable hooks
- ✓ Paper clips
- ✓ Clothesline and pins

- ✓ Two-sided tape
- ✓ Highlight tape
- ✓ Wikki Stix
- ✓ Correction tape
- ✓ Notebook rings
- ✓ String
- ✓ Rubber bands

Teach the Children to Use the Activities Successfully

Here are a few tips to teach the children to use the materials successfully:

- ✓ Make the activity self-checking. It does not matter if the child peeks at the answer. Working and reworking the activity is what reinforces learning.

- ✓ Put the activity in a low-traffic area. The children will work with less distraction there. It does not have to be a large area, just in an out-of-the-way place.

- ✓ Make the system self-managing by limiting the number of children using the activity at the one time. Let's take an example. Let's assume you want to limit the number of children using an activity to two. Place a library pocket nearby the activity. Have all the children's names on jumbo craft sticks; store them in an orange juice can.
Write "2" on the pocket (the "2" means that only two children can work there). When a child wants to work the activity, he removes his name from the orange juice can and places it in the library pocket. When there are two sticks in the pocket, the activity is full.

- ✓ Change an activity when you observe that most of the children are misusing it. It usually means that they are bored with it. Put out something new. When an activity is not being chosen, put it away. Take it out six weeks later. The children will like seeing an "old friend"; others will be ready for it that was not ready for it six weeks earlier.

Teach the Children to Work Independently

Train the children to use an activity successfully. Let's use a poem chart as an example; let's focus on keywords (keywords are the words you want the children to learn to read, to say, and to recognize). So, what do you need to do for the children to be successful? Here's a sequence.

- ✓ Read and re-read the poem aloud with the group until all the children know it.
- ✓ Move from the spoken words to pictures of keywords; pictures of what the words are describing. If the word says "apple," for example, have a picture of an apple. Display the poem chart. The children will associate the word with a picture of it.
- ✓ Once the children know the poem and the keywords, move to written words of the picture. Set the pictures aside; have the children match the written words to keywords in the poem. Have them place the written words over the keywords in the poem.
- ✓ When the children understand matching the written word to the keywords in the poem, cover the keywords with masking tape; have the children find the keywords written on cards and place them in each "missing word" spot in the poem.
- ✓ Model how to move the words and the sentence segments on the poem chart. This builds interest and enthusiasm. The children observe how to do the poem chart successfully. The children themselves become models for the other children. They will show each other.
- ✓ Have several of the children model how to use the moveable parts of the poem chart. Let them show what they know. You'll find out if they really do understand how you expect

them to use it. Such insights are especially useful when you are occupied in another corner of the room while they are working with interactive stuff elsewhere.
- ✓ Place the poem chart in an independent work area for the children. They really will do it all by themselves.

How to Store All of the Interactive Stuff

Storage is a universal problem for teachers. There is no easy solution. For small things, I have found that copy-paper boxes work well. Label the contents, or the topic, in an easy-to-see place. That way, you won't have to take the boxes down to know what's inside them. Write a more detailed contents list on the inside of the box lid. Store the activities topically, or in an interactive-games box. Box storage can be under tables, or use the boxes as learning-center dividers. If you have an empty closet, cabinets, or shelves you are fortunate.

The hardest objects to store are the large posters and charts. I have found several approaches useful. Cut the posters into three equal sections; tape the sections back together. Apply tape on the back and the front of the chart leaving two clear seams dividing the sections. Fold the charts along the clear seams. This approach makes charts and posters easy to fold and store (please see the drawing below).

- ✓ Purchase commercially made artist's portfolios, or use chart boxes.
- ✓ Use coat hangers on a pocket-chart stand. Attach the charts to the hangers with clothespins.
- ✓ Purchase an over-the-door clothes rack; use coat hangers and pins to hang the charts.
- ✓ A skirt hanger is useful to hang charts. It is flat; the posters can be tiered when attached to the hanger with the clothespins built into the hanger.
- ✓ Have a print shop bind the charts together.
- ✓ Purchase commercially made, large resealable "baggies" (for flat storage).
- ✓ Use two large ceiling hooks (the kind to hang-up bicycles in your garage, for example). Put up the hooks, and punch holes in the top of the charts the same distance as between the hooks; attach notebook rings in the holes and hang charts over the ceiling hooks. To remove a poster, open the ring and remove the poster.

You win the battle of storage by improvising within the space you have. Imagination helps.

If you run across better solutions to the quest for more storage space, be sure to share it with others. Me first! E-mail me at my website sharonmacdonald.com.

1. Watermelon Pie

Adapted from <u>Alligator Pie</u> by Dennis Lee
By Sharon MacDonald

Watermelon Pie!
Watermelon Pie!
If I don't get some
I think I'm going to cry.
You can take away my shirt
And take away my tie,
But please don't take
My Watermelon Pie!

Alligator Cake!
Alligator Cake!
If I don't get some
I think I'm going to break.
You can take away my frog
And take away my snake,
But please don't take
My Alligator Cake!

Huckleberry Bread!
Huckleberry Bread!
If I don't get some
I think I'm going to bed
You can take away my leg
And take away my head.
But please don't take
My Huckleberry Bread!

Snicker Doodle Torte!
Snicker Doodle Torte!
If I don't get some
I think I'm going to snort.
You can take away my Carl
And take away my Mort.
But please don't take
My Snicker Doodle Torte!

Activities:

1. Have sentence strips available so the children can dictate to you new verses to *Watermelon Pie*. For children who are writing, put left over sentence strips in a basket with markers. Encourage the children to write their own verses.

2. Collect pie tins. Cut out red paper circles to cover the bottoms of the tins. Draw watermelon seeds on the circles and glue them to the inside bottoms of the pie tins. Have the children clap the tins together as they say the poem. Older children can make their own *Watermelon Pie* cymbals!

3. Have the children draw pictures of some of the themes in the poem. For example, have them draw a watermelon pie; then, have them draw their versions of a man's tie, a shirt, and a crying child. Have the children cut out what they have drawn and glue it to card stock. Laminate them. Place their work in a basket next to the poem. As each child reads the poem, have him put his drawn picture over the word describing it. If the poem is on the wall, place a small ball of *Sticky Tac* nearby so the picture will stay in place when the child sticks it up over the word.

4. Make a poem chart. Have index cards available for the children to write the rhyming words from the song. After they have made their rhyming word cards, have them match the words to the poem chart. If they cannot write, write the rhyming words for them. Put the rhyming words in a basket below the poem chart. Have the children match them.

2. The Crayon Box
By Sharon MacDonald

I draw with orange.
Make a line of blue,
A circle of yellow,
And red dots or two.
I zigzag with purple.
Make loops of green.
Then back in the box
Go my colors of dreams.

Activities:

1. Purchase six sheets of transparency film and a set of primary- and secondary color permanent markers. On the first sheet of film, draw an orange crescent like the one below. On the second sheet, draw a short, blue line. On the third, draw a large yellow circle; on the fourth draw two large red circles; color them solid. On the fifth, make a zigzag across the top of the circle with the purple marker. On the last sheet, draw two loops like the pattern below. As you say the poem, layer the sheets sequentially on an overhead, start with the crescent and end with the face.

2. Make a puff book. Fold, open, cut, re-fold, and puff into a book the poem sheet on page 16. Follow the directions below.

1. Fold the page like a hamburger.

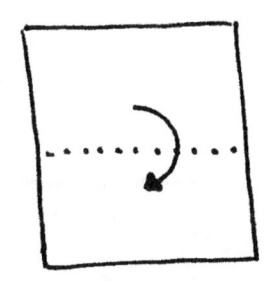

2. Fold the half sheet like a hot dog.

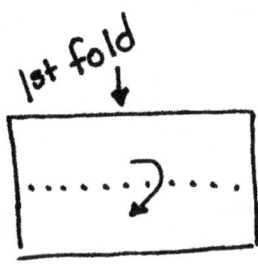

3. Fold the hot dog in half to make a burrito.

4. Unfold 2nd fold to the 1st fold. Make sure the 1st fold is at the top.

Cut from the 1st fold to the 2nd fold.

5. Unfold the page.

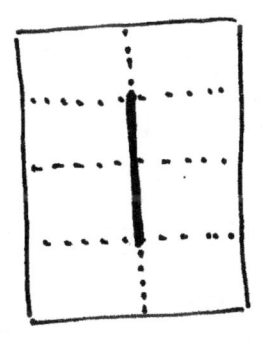

6. Fold into a hot dog.

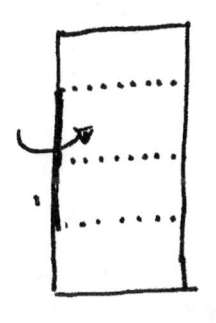

You will be Folding over the cut slit.

7. Puff the book by pushing on both ends forcing the center to puff out!

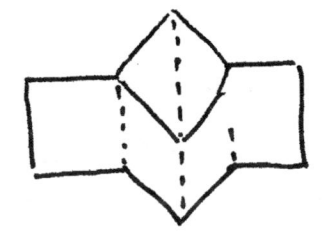

8. Fold your book.

15

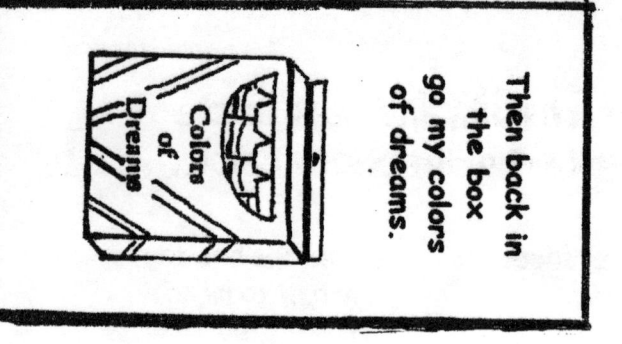

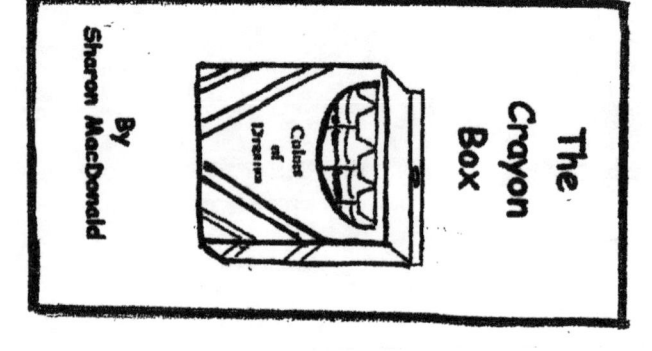

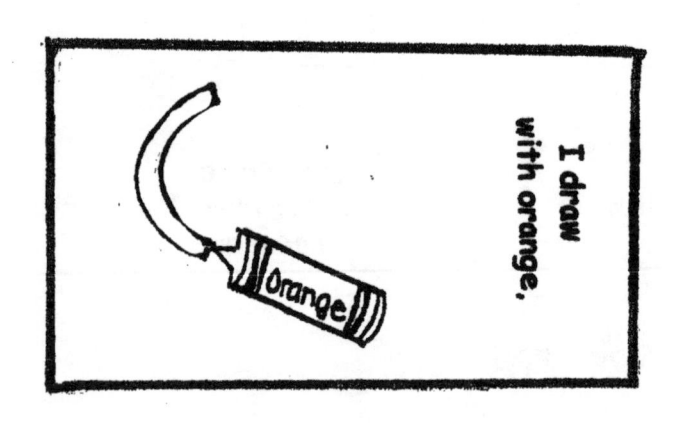

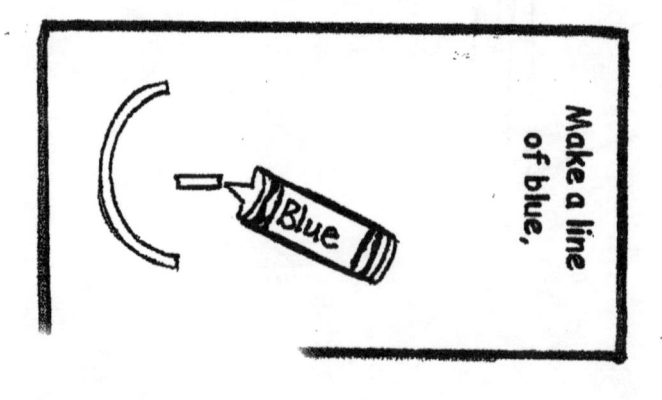

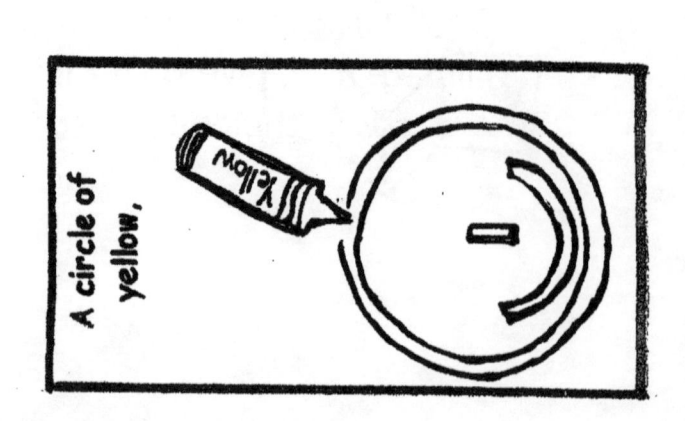

The Crayon Box By Sharon MacDonald	Then back in the box go my colors of dreams.
I draw with orange,	
Make a line of blue,	A circle of yellow,
And red dots, or two.	
I zigzag with purple,	
Make loops of green.	

16

3. Zip Up Your Jacket
Adapted by Sharon MacDonald

Zip up your jacket
Put on your cap
Old Mr. South Wind
Is taking a nap.
But,
Mr. North Wind
Will nip at your nose
And freeze your fingers
And your toes.
So....

Zip up your jacket
Put on your cap
Let Mr. South Wind
Take an old nap.
And,
Mr. North Wind
Can nip at our nose
We'll cover our fingers
And our toes.
Burrrr!

Activities:

1. Make a poem chart on a large sheet of poster board. Laminate it. Have the children put *Wikki Stix* around all of the words in the poem that rhyme.

2. Fill a large basket with winter clothes; like jackets with zippers, scarves, gloves, mittens, caps, and boots. Have the children dress for winter as you sing the poem.

3. Make a poem chart by copying the poem on a large sheet of paper. Laminate it. Place a basket of magnetic letters and a magnet board beside the chart. The children use the letters to make the words in the poem.

4. Place a jacket with a zippered-front over a straight-back chair so that a child can sit in the chair, attach the zipper, and zip-up the jacket.

5. Pair-up the children; have them take turns dressing each other in winter clothes. Use a stopwatch and time how long it takes for each child to dress for winter.

4. Peanut Brown
By Sharon MacDonald

I'm a little peanut brown,
Growing 'neath the dark, dark ground.
Someone came and pulled me up,
Now I'm just some sticky stuff.
Peanut brown, (crack, crack)
From the ground, (crack, crack)
Someone found, (crack, crack),
And mashed around, (crack, crack)
Peanut Butter!

I'm a little peanut _____,
Growing 'neath the dark, dark _____.
Someone came and pulled me ____,
Now I'm just some sticky _____.
Peanut brown, (crack, crack)
From the _____ (crack, crack)
Someone _____ (crack, crack)
And mashed _____ (crack, crack)
Peanut _____!

Activities:

1. Sing this to the song *I'm a Little Acorn Brown*.

2. During the second verse, allow the children to speak the missing words. Copy the poem on a large chart and attach a soft-side Velcro strip in the blank word-spaces. Place a hook-side Velcro strip on the back of the words that belong in the blanks. Have the children put the words in the blanks (please use the words on pages 20 and 21).

brown

ground

up

stuff

ground

found

around

Butter!

3. Use the picture directions below to make peanut-butter-and-jelly sandwiches with the children.

Peanut Butter and Jelly Sandwich

1. Spread peanut butter on the bread.

2. Spread the jelly on the bread.

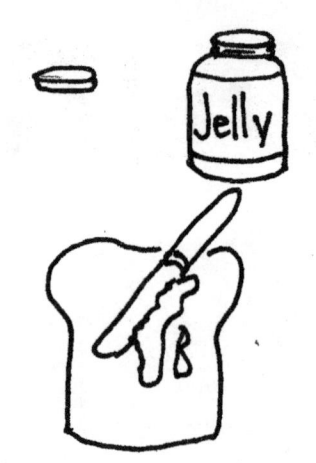

3. Close the sandwich

4. Eat!

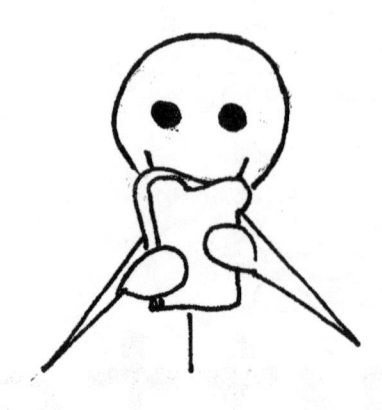

4. Use the picture directions below to have the children crack-and-shell peanuts.

Shelling Peanuts

1. Crack the peanuts open.

2. Take out the peanuts.

3. Share with a friend.

4. Eat!

5. Little Tree House
By Sharon MacDonald

Please build for me
A house in a tree
Called the little tree house,
The little tree house.

I'd like to be
In a house in a tree
Called the little tree house,
The little tree house.

Simplest thing.
There isn't much to it.
You just climb a tree
And nail everything to it.

I'd like it so,
Wherever I'd go,
I'd sing of my
Little tree house.

Activities:
1. Have the children draw a tree house.

2. Use the movements below with the poem.

3. Have the children build a tree house with blocks or *Legos*.

4. Find the contractions in the poem.

I'd = I would

isn't = is not

Repeat the following movements throughout the poem as you say it:

Tap your knees with your hands two times.
Clap your hands two times.
Snap; then, Clap your hands two times;
Touch your nose with your right hand; then, reach across your body to touch your left shoulder.
With your left hand, touch your nose; then, reach across to touch your Right shoulder.
Touch your thumbs to your fingers three times

5. Make a paper-bag "tree" as you read the poem. Here's how. Open a brown lunch bag; keep the bottom flat. Twist the middle of the bag into a tree "trunk." Tear downward, about four inches from the top of the bag, in eight places, the same distance apart. You will have 10 narrow strips. Twist the strips into tree "branches" (please see the picture directions below). Challenge the children by asking them to think about things they could put in the tree to make a tree house.

(Note: A special thanks to Dr. Jean Feldman for this activity).

Step 1   Step 2   Step 3

6. Sing a Song of Apples
By Sharon MacDonald

Sing a song of *apples*,
Apples full of *seeds*;
Apples that are *round* and *red*,
And grow on *apple trees*.

Apples make great *applesauce*,
And *juice* that you should try.
My favorite way of eating them
Is in an *apple pie!*

Activities:

1. This poem can be sung to the tune of *Sing a Song of Six Pence*.

2. For children, who need the concrete experiences, examine apples by feeling, smelling, measuring, and weighing them. Cut different varieties of apples in halves and quarters (use *Red- and Yellow Delicious*, and *Granny Smith*). Examine the inside and the seeds.

Compare the taste. After the children understand the properties of apples, have them make applesauce and taste apple juice. Maybe they can even help you bake an apple pie.

3. Have the children do a picture-word match. Here's how.

Step 1: Write each line of the song on a sentence strip. Make a pocket-over-the-word by cutting a strip of leftover laminating film to fit the word; use clear-plastic tape to attach the film over the word. Apply the tape along the bottom and each side of the laminating film (please see the directions below).

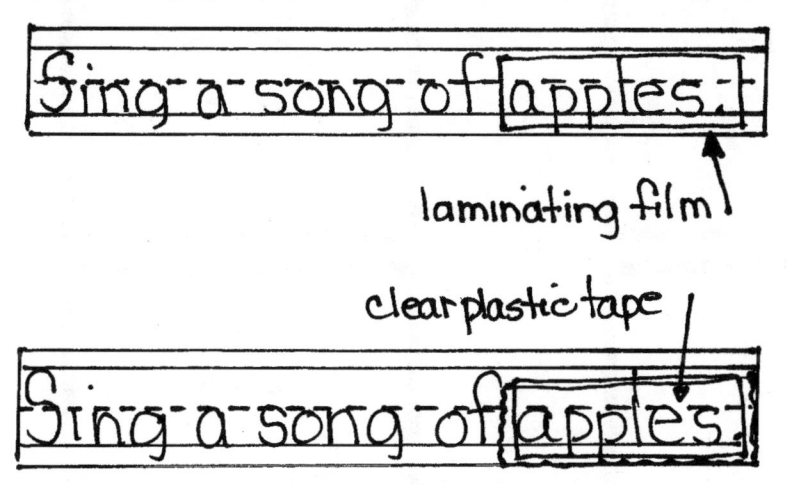

Sing a song of apples.

laminating film

clear plastic tape

Sing a song of apples.

Step 2: Copy and cut out the apple pattern below. Trace the pattern on red construction paper. Make eight, red-paper apples.

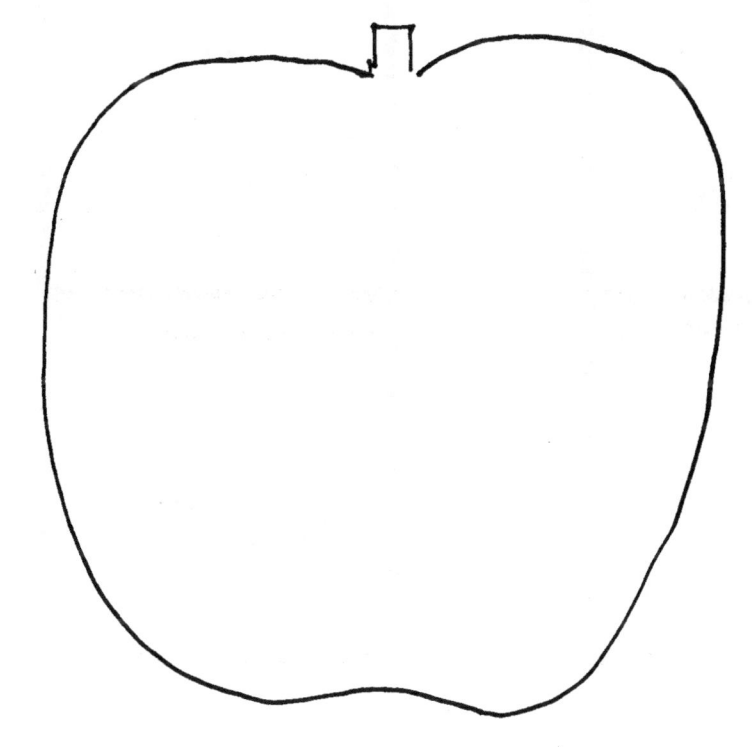

Step 3: Copy, color, and cut out the key apple pictures below. Glue each picture to one of the red paper apples. The children match the apples to the words by placing them in the laminating-film pockets.

apples	seeds
round	red
apple trees	applesauce
juice	apple pie

28

Step 4: Copy, color, back with construction paper, and laminate the picture direction below. Place it with the poem chart. Encourage the children to use the picture-direction card and work the activity independently.

Sing a Song of Apples Picture Directions

Sing a song of apples,
Apples full of seeds;
Apples that are round and red,
And grow on apple trees.
Apples make great applesauce,
And juice that you should try.
My favorite way of eating them
Is in an apple pie!

As you say the poem match the apples to the words!

4. If the children are working at a more challenging level, have them match the words to the words in the poem. Write the key words on sentence strips; cut each word from the strip.

Note: Key words are the italicized words in the poem. They are the words you want to focus on. Key words in this activity are: Apples, seeds, red, round, apple trees, applesauce, juice, and apple pie.

5. To challenge the children more, write the poem on sentence strips. Leave out the key words. Write the key words on another sentence strip; cut each word from the strip. Have the children fill-in the missing word with the key words cut from the sentence strip.

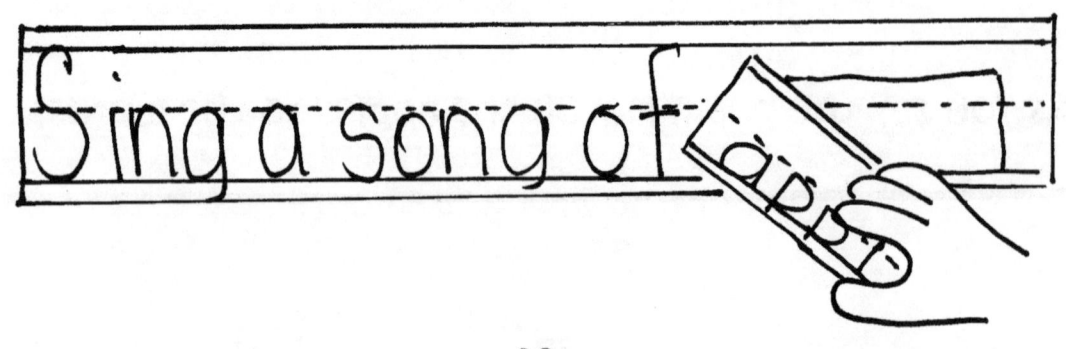

7. Painting
By Sharon MacDonald

I'm picky with my painting
Because I want to see,
The colors brushed on paper
In a way that pleases me.
I love to paint my own thing
To see what I can do;
It doesn't have to have an end;
I stop, when I am through.

Drip, drop, splash, drop, dribble drop, do!
Drip, drop, splash, drop, dribble drop, do!
Drip, drop, splash, drop, dribble drop, do!
I paint the whole page,
And I stop when I 'm through!

When all the page is painted
And it's set aside to dry,
I feel so warm and wonderful
But please don't ask me why.

The way I feel when painting
I can only tell a little;
You start, then, you end,
But the fun is in the middle.

Drip, drop, splash, drop, dribble drop, do!
Drip, drop, splash, drop, dribble drop, do!
Drip, drop, splash, drop, dribble drop, do!
I paint the whole page
And I stop when I 'm through!

Activities:

1. This poem can be sung to the tune of *Down In the Meadow, In An Itty Bitty Pond*.

2. This is an activity for children working on consonant blends. Provide three colors of highlight tape. Have them use the first color to place a piece over the words that begin with "dr." Have them use the second color to tape over the word that begins with "br." Use the third color to tape over the words that begin with "spl."

3. This is an activity for younger children. Make a poem poster. Place a highlight-tape color card next to the poem poster (a highlight-tape color card lets you reuse the tape over again). To make the color card, attach pieces of highlight tape to a laminated index-card (please see below).

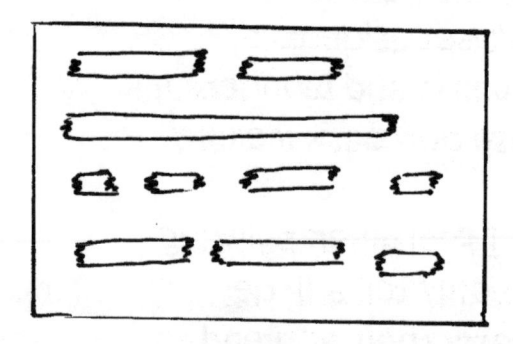

Have the children peel off a strip of tape and place it over the word "paint" each time they find it. When they have completed the task, remove the tape and save it on the laminated index card.

To expand the activity, select any letter or combination of letters, for the children to highlight with tape.

4. Have the children explore two activities: painting-with-water colors-on-a-flat-surface; and, tempera-painting-at-an-easel. With each activity, let them paint on a variety of surfaces; like, brown grocery bags, newspaper, cardboard, corrugated cardboard, gift wrapping scraps, cereal boxes, cheesecloth, wax-, sand-, and graph paper, thin wood sheets, and leftover, laminating film.

5. Ask the children questions like these as they paint:

> - What do you see when you paint?
> - How do you know you are finished painting?
> - What do you like the most about painting?
> - What do you like the least about it?
> - What does painting sound like?
> - Why do you think people have painted for many years on different surfaces?
> - What is your recipe for making paint?
> - What is your favorite paint color?
> - What other ways do people use paint?
> - What colors mix well together?
> - Why does paint dry?
> - How many colors did you use?
> - How many colors did you make when you painted?
> - What happens when you use a thin brush to paint, rather than a thick one?

6. Have the children put on old shirts, back-side-front; take them outside. Put out several long sheets of butcher paper; hold down the sheet corners with rocks. Give each child a small paper cup of liquid tempera-paint and a paintbrush. Ask each child to dribble-drop the paint on the butcher paper. Encourage them to trade colors. As the paintings dry, talk about Jackson Pollock's painting. In the 1950s, he made drips, dribbles, and drops famous, splashing paint on canvas. His style was called Abstract Expressionism.

NOTE: To protect the children's shoes from the dribbles and drops, have them bring from home two pairs of old socks. Use one pair of socks to slide on over the children's shoes and up their legs. Be sure to tuck-in long pants into the sock tubes. Cut off at the ankle the other pair. Toss away the foot piece; slide the tubes over the children's wrists and up their arms. Tuck long sleeves into the tube ends.

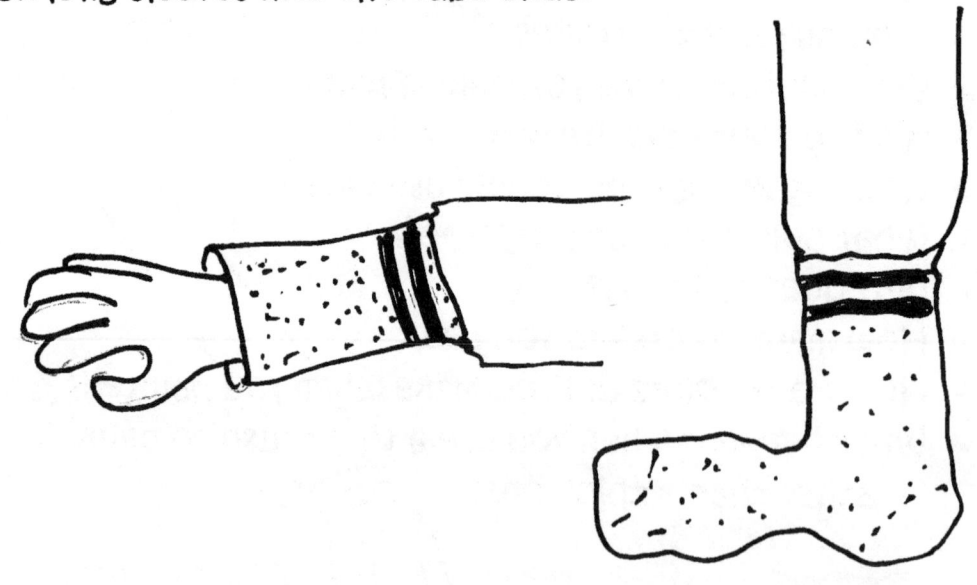

7. Make a poem book illustrated with the children's paintings.

Step 1. Collect: 25 sheets of 18" x 24" construction paper, 3 notebook rings, 24 sentence strips. Gather a few children to work at the easel.

Step 2. Write one line of the poem on a sentence strip.

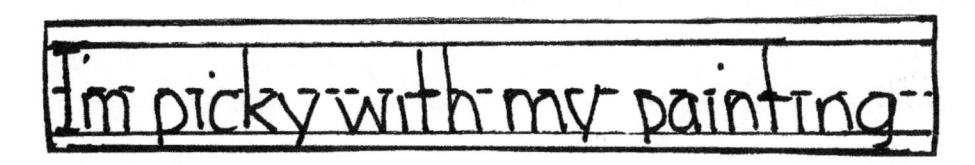

I'm picky with my painting

Note: Because the last two lines of the chorus are short, I put both on one sentence strip ("I paint the whole page and I stop when I'm through").

Step 3. Glue each line of the poem along the 24" bottom of the construction paper.

Step 4. Have the children paint at the easel; have each child choose one painting for inclusion in the poem book and trim it to fit above one of the sentence strips.

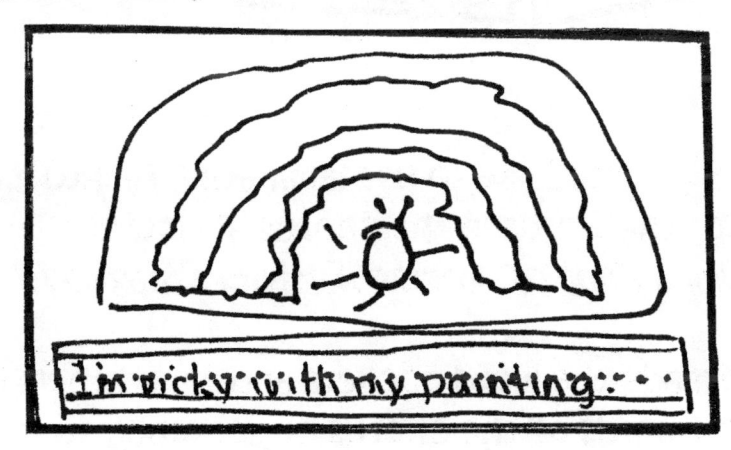

I'm picky with my painting

Step 5. After each child has contributed one painting, and each page has a painting with a line of the poem, laminate each page of the poem book.

Step 6. Have the children help you design the cover. Let them tell you what to write for the title, author, and illustrators. After that has been decided, have each child choose a paint color, then, dip his thumb, and make a thumb print on the cover. After all the prints have dried, have each child return to sign his name under his thumbprint.

Step 7. Laminate the cover.

Step 8. Put the book together. Punch holes in each page and bind with notebook rings.

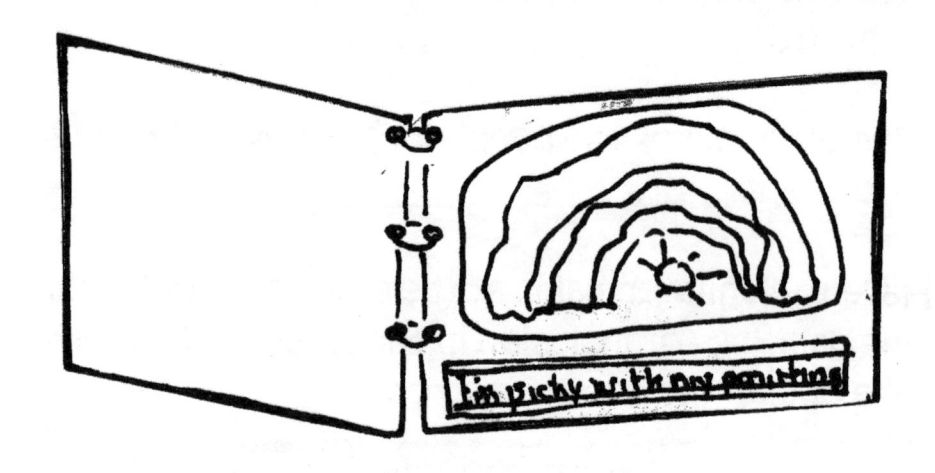

Alternative: If you would like to use laminating film to make clear pockets for the words in the chorus, follow the directions in *Sing a Song of Apples*, Activity 3, page 27.

After you have made the word pockets and taped them in place, put all the words of the chorus on sentence strips. Cut the words from the strips. Store them in a resealable baggie. Have the children match the words on the sentence strip segments to the words in the chorus by slipping them into the pockets over the words.

8. Up and Down
By Sharon MacDonald

Up and down are places
That I'm supposed to know;
Just like in and out,
Off and on, and high and low.
But I've noticed when I get there,
All tired and out of breath,
There's just another up and down
To other places left!

Chorus:
Up and down, high and low,
Off and on, fast and slow,
Back and forth, big and small,
Here and there, short and tall.

Quieter:
But I've noticed when I get there,
All tired and out of breath,
There's just another up and down
To other places left!

Fade away:
Up and down, high and low,
Off and on, fast and slow,
Back and forth, big and small,
Here and there, short and tall.

Activities:

1. Write the poem on a chart. Have the children use a read-the-room pointer to point to the words that are opposites.

Here are some room-pointer ideas:
- Use a stuffed garden glove with the pinkie-, ring-, and middle fingers glued down to the palm of the glove; leave the thumb and index finger up, pointed toward the sky. The index finger is used for pointing. Stuff the glove with cotton or old stockings. Slip the glove on a dowel and hot glue it in place. After the glue has dried, tie a big ribbon around the glove cuff to gather the glove around the dowel.
- Try a plastic apple with a hole in the bottom. Put the apple on a dowel and hot glue it in place. Point with the apple.
- Use a star, or other shape, cut from a plastic, disposable plate; decorated with glitter on both sides. Hot glue the star to a yardstick.
- Try any shape. Attach any shape with a brad to a gift-wrap roll. Point with it.

2. Have the children talk with the other children about words that are opposites. Ask them to make an *Opposites Chart*. Write down their dictation of opposite words. Place the chart where the children can see it. Have them add to it when they think of a pair of opposite words.

3. Have the children think of other poems. Ask them to make the sound fade at the end, just like in the *Up and Down* poem. Talk about how sounds gets fainter, and more difficult to hear, as a person moves away from the source of the sound.

9. Here is a Bunny
By Sharon MacDonald

Here is a bunny with ears so funny
And here is a place that he found.
With his feet and his hands he digs in the sand
Makes a home in a hole in the ground.

Here is a bunny with ears so funny
And here is a carrot to eat.
With a munch and a crunch he nibbles his lunch
And slides down the hole on his feet.

Here is a bunny with ears so funny
And here is a log in his path.
With a bump, then a jump, he lands with a thump
And goes on his way with a laugh, ha ha!

Activities:

1. Make bunny "ears" by collecting two fabric shoulder-pads, scissors, a one-inch-thick headband, and a hot glue gun. Cut two slits on each side of the two pads. Slide the headband into each shoulder-pad. When you have them in place, use the hot-glue gun to squeeze glue into each slit. Hold the ears firmly until the glue dries. (Note: This helps hold the ears upright on the headband; please see the illustration on page 40.)

Step 1 Cut slits in the shoulder pads.

Step 2. Slide the shoulder pads onto the headband.

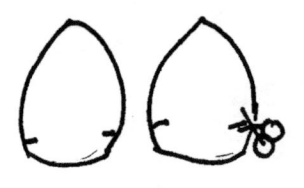

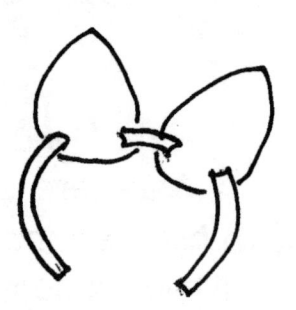

Step 3 Use a hot glue gun and squirt glue into each slit.

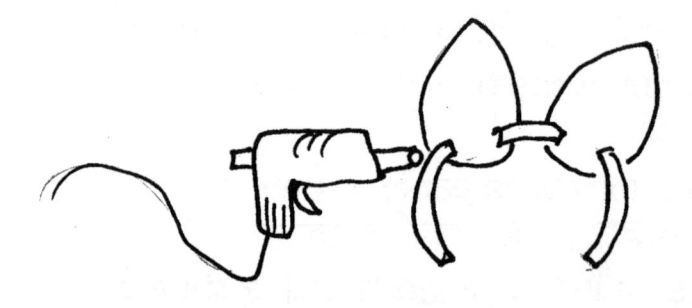

2. Make a "tail" for the bunny. Make a large, pink pompom and attach it to a piece of elastic long enough to go around a child's waist. Have a child put on the tail, and the ears to be a bunny.

3. Write the poem on a large chart. Give the children *Wikki Stixs* and scissors. The children can find all the rhyming words and use *Wikki Stixs* to outline the words. If the children can write, have them write all the words that they have circled on index cards. Encourage them to work with a friend and have their friend match all the writing words to the poster.

40

4. The children can "read" the instructions below to dress like a bunny.

Be a Bunny

You need:

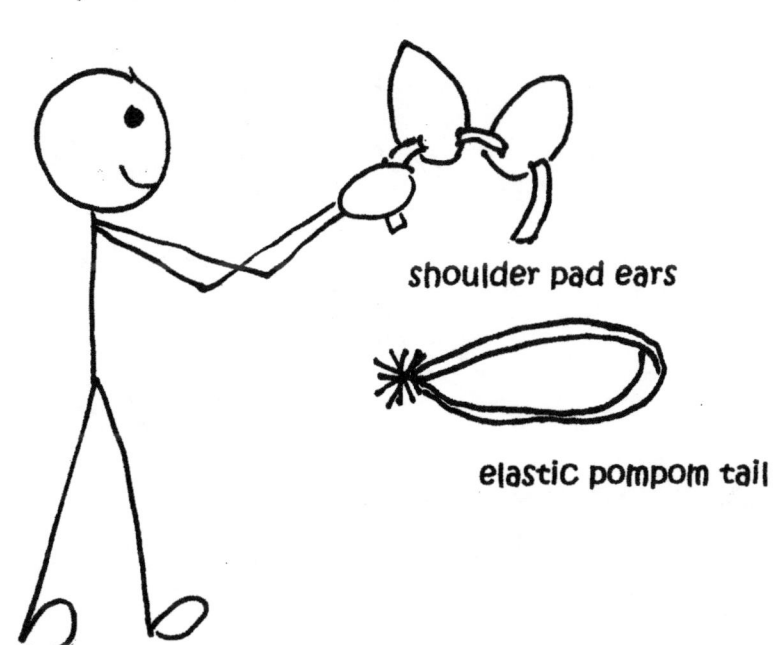

shoulder pad ears

elastic pompom tail

1. Put on the ears.

2. Put on the tail.

3. Hop like a bunny.

41

5. Have carrots for snack. Allow the children to help you wash and peel them (please see the picture directions below).

Carrot Medallions

1. Wash the carrot with a vegetable brush.

2. Peel the carrot with a carrot peeler.

3. Slice the carrots into medallions.

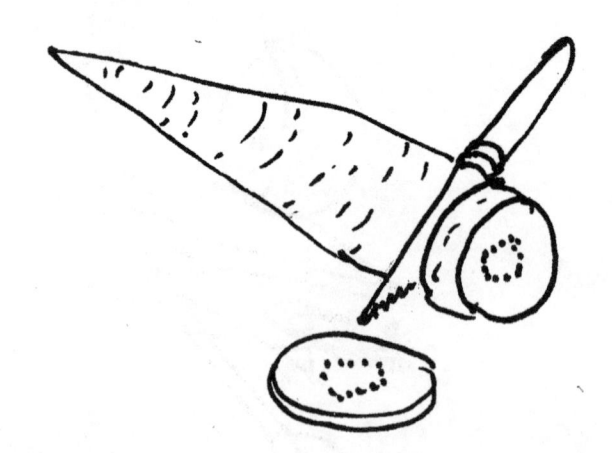

4. Eat!

10. Crayons
By Sharon MacDonald

Oh, I wish I had a little red jug
To put my crayons in.
I'd take them out, go scribble, scribble, scribble,
And put them back again.

Oh, I wish I had a little purple car
To put my crayons in.
I'd take them out and draw a line,
And put them back again.

Oh, I wish I had a little yellow sun
To put my crayons in.
I'd take them out, draw 'round and 'round,
And put them back again.

Oh, I wish I had a little blue cloud
To put my crayons in.
I'd take them out, go dot, dot, dot,
And put them back again.

Oh, I wish I had a little orange ball
To put my crayons in.
I'd take them out, go bounce, bounce, bounce,
And put them back again.

Oh, I've got myself a little green box
To put my crayons in.
I'll take them out and count them all,
And put them back again.

Activities:

1. Sing the poem to the song *Polly Wolly Doodle All Day*.

2. Give each child a box of crayons, and a large sheet of paper. Have them draw with the crayons as you read the poem. Encourage them to make scribbles, draw lines, make circular motions and dots, and bounce the crayon on the paper as the poem describes.

3. Copy, color, back with construction paper, laminate, and cut out all the key drawings that will be used in the poem (please see the drawings below). Place a small piece of hook-side Velcro on the back of each drawing. Copy the poem on a poster-board sheet and laminate it. Put a piece of soft-side Velcro next to each line of the poem that has a word that matches a drawing. When the children read the poem, have them place each drawing next to the line with the word the drawing depicts.

jug	sun	ball
car	cloud	box

4. Make multiple copies of page 47, *Paper Crayons*. Use the copies to do any of the following activities:

- ✓ Write the numbers 1 to 10 (or 1-20, 1-50, 1-100) on the paper crayons. Have the children put them in numerical order.
- ✓ Write the color words on the paper crayons. Do not color the crayon. Color another paper crayon a corresponding color. Have the children match the colored paper crayon to the paper crayon with the correct word written on it.
- ✓ Color the paper crayons and write the color words on them. Tape them to blocks in the Block Center so the children can make a house of colors.
- ✓ Shrink or enlarge the copies; make 6-8 different-size sets. Have the children put them in order by size.
- ✓ Use the crayons to make nametags.
- ✓ Make a color, concentration game.
- ✓ Write expressions on the crayon sheets like: "...in the pink," "...green with envy," "...feeling blue," or "...black as pitch." What do the children think they mean?
- ✓ Find rhyming words for the colors you are using. For example: write red, black, yellow, blue, and green; one word per paper crayon. Match them with bed, back, fellow, true, and queen on another set of paper crayons. The children match the rhyming words to the colors.
- ✓ Make several photocopies of the crayon page and color them as follows: 6 blue, 6 red, 6 yellow, 6 orange, 6 purple and 6 green. Encourage the children to make 2-, 3-, or 4 patterns-in-a-sequence using the colors.
- ✓ Write the color words on the paper crayons (red, yellow, blue, purple, orange, and green) and color them the same color. Have the children put the crayon colors words in alphabetical order.

✓ Make a color word *Bingo* game. Follow the step-by-step directions below.

Step 1: Make four *Bingo* boards like the examples below. Make a board with 25 squares on it. Write "Free" on the square in the middle. Use the color words in a box of 24 crayons.

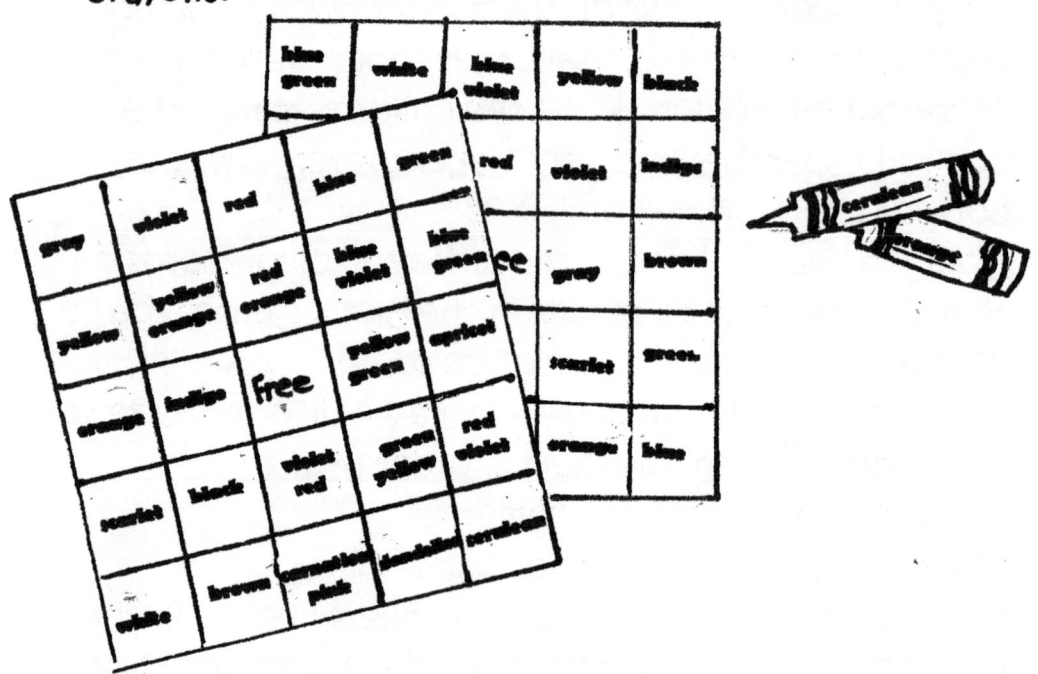

Step 2: Make the calling cards by using the color words in a box of 24 crayons. Write each color word on a paper crayon.

Step 3: Give each child playing the game a box of 24 crayons. The crayons will be used like *Bingo* chips to cover the color words as they are called.

Step 4: When a child has a row of crayons horizontally, vertically, or diagonally across the board, have him say, *"Bingo."*

Paper Crayons

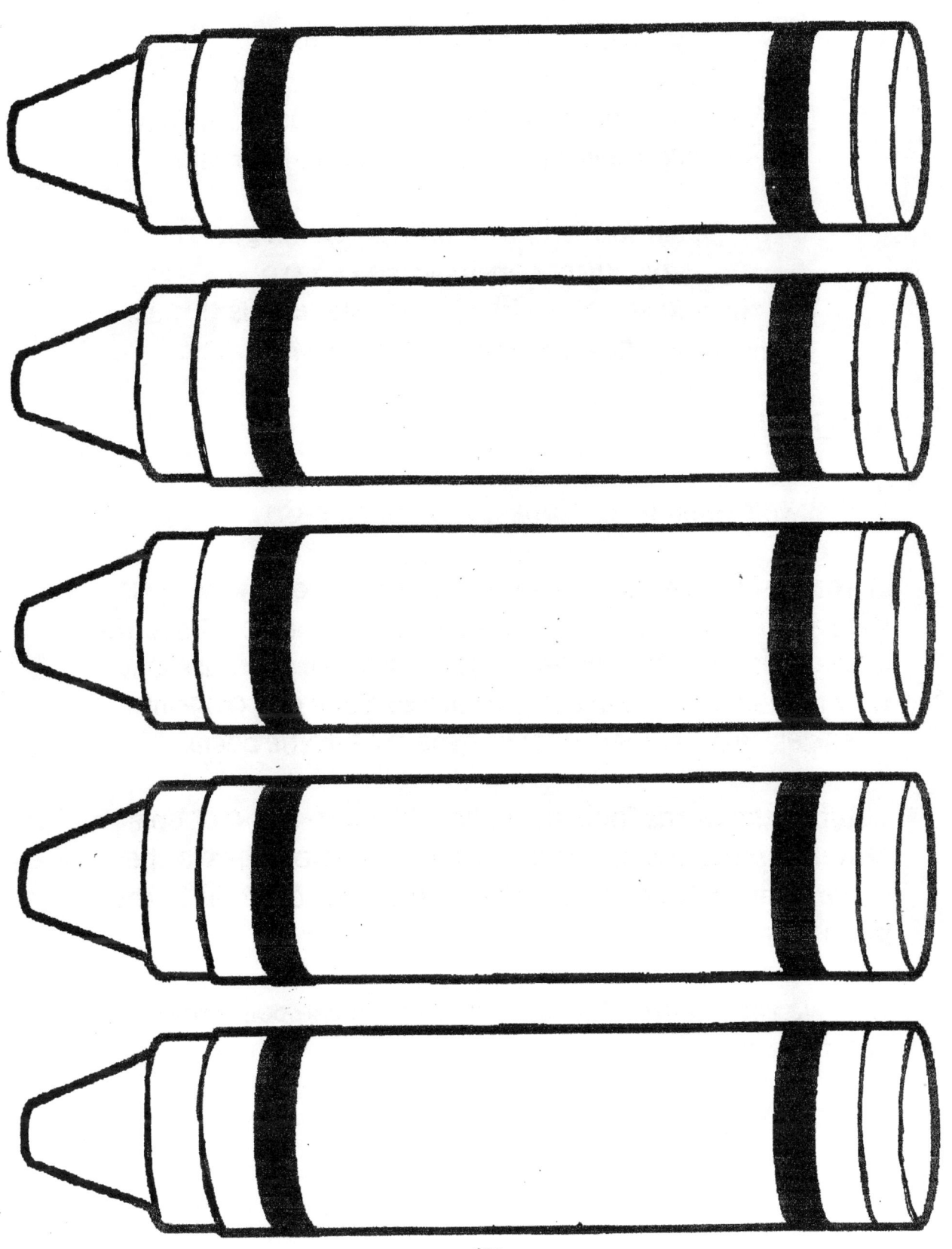

11. Six Little Frogs
By Sharon MacDonald

Six little frogs that I once knew;
Green ones, brown ones, red ones, too.
But the one bullfrog with the freckles on his throat,
He ruled them all with a croak, croak, croak.

Down to the blue pond they would go;
Hop, jump, hop, jump, to and fro.
But the one bullfrog with the freckles on his throat,
He ruled them all with a croak, croak, croak.

Activities:

1. Sing this poem to the song *Six Little Ducks*.

2. Make six, paper-bag puppets in the shape of a frog. Use the pattern and the directions on pages 49 and 50. Place them in the Music or Library Center for the children to use when they read or sing the poem. Be sure to make one frog--with "freckles on his throat"--just like the frog in the poem.

3. Write the words "hop, jump, hop, jump, to and fro" on a sentence strip; cut out each word with scissors. Have the children put the words together in the same order as in the poem.

4. Have the children find all the words in the poem that describe color.

Directions:
1. Color the frog pieces
2. Cut out the eyes, face, and body.
3. Glue the eyes on the frog face.
4. Glue the head on the top of the lunch bag.
5. Glue the body inside the fold of the top of the lunch bag and to the lunch bag. Make sure the mouth is in the fold. Please, see the directions below.

49

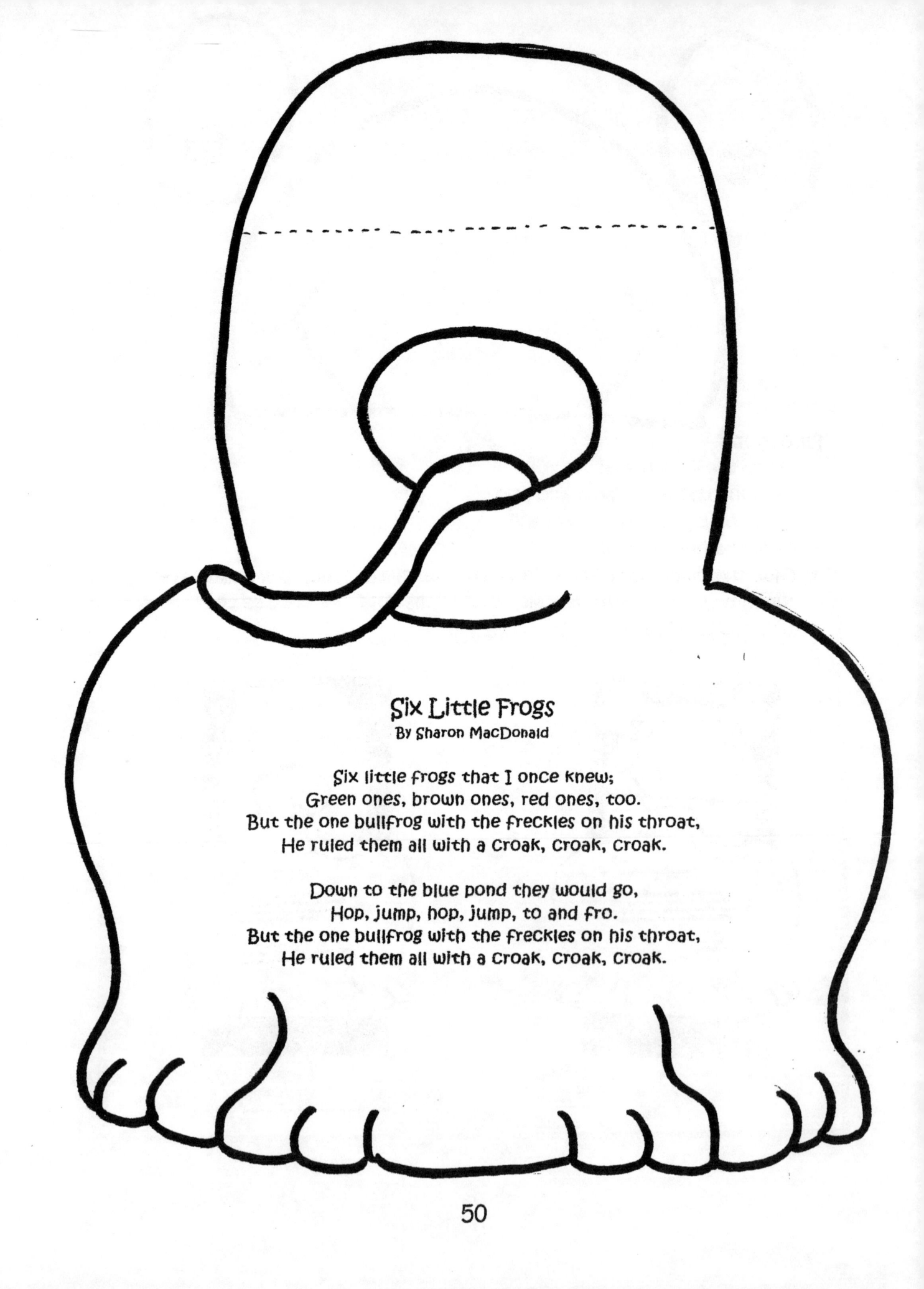

Six Little Frogs
By Sharon MacDonald

Six little frogs that I once knew;
Green ones, brown ones, red ones, too.
But the one bullfrog with the freckles on his throat,
He ruled them all with a Croak, Croak, Croak.

Down to the blue pond they would go,
Hop, jump, hop, jump, to and fro.
But the one bullfrog with the freckles on his throat,
He ruled them all with a Croak, Croak, Croak.

5. Write the "long-O" and the "short-O" words on index cards. Place them in a basket and have the children sort them by the sound.

6. Use the cards below to make a set of frog-life-cycle sequence cards. Color and cut out the cards. Back them with construction paper and laminate them. Please see the pictures below. Follow the directions on page 53 to make a sequence board. The children use the sequence board to put the cards in order. Put the activity, the picture directions (shown on page 53), and the sequence board on a tray for the children to work. Store the cards and the board in a small sandwich bag.

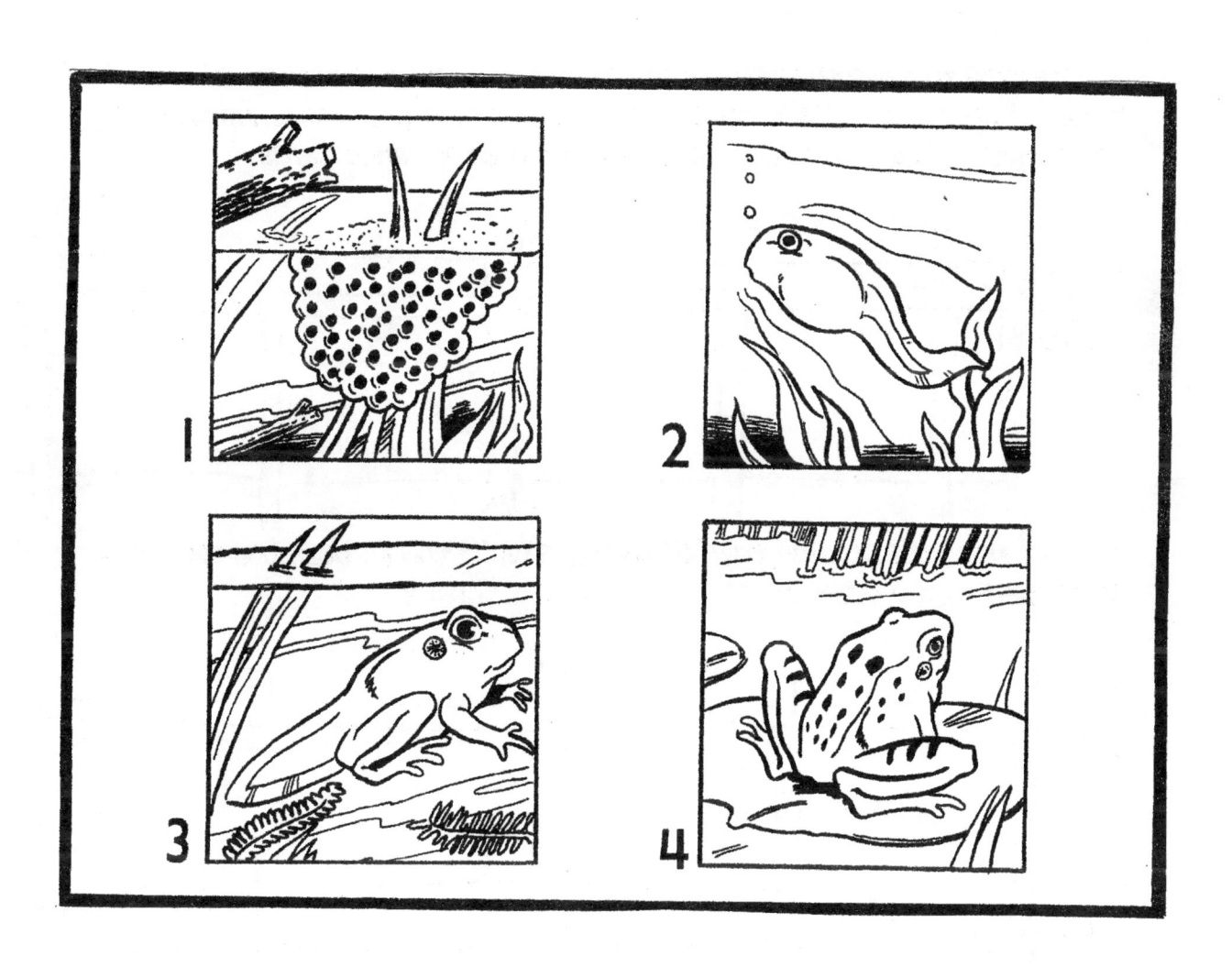

Sequence Card Base

You need a 4" x 18" strip of white plastic garbage bag, a roll of colored tape, scissors, and a black marker.

1. Lay the garbage bag section on a table. Use tape to mark off the boxes. Tape the bag to the table as you work so it will not move as you make the base.

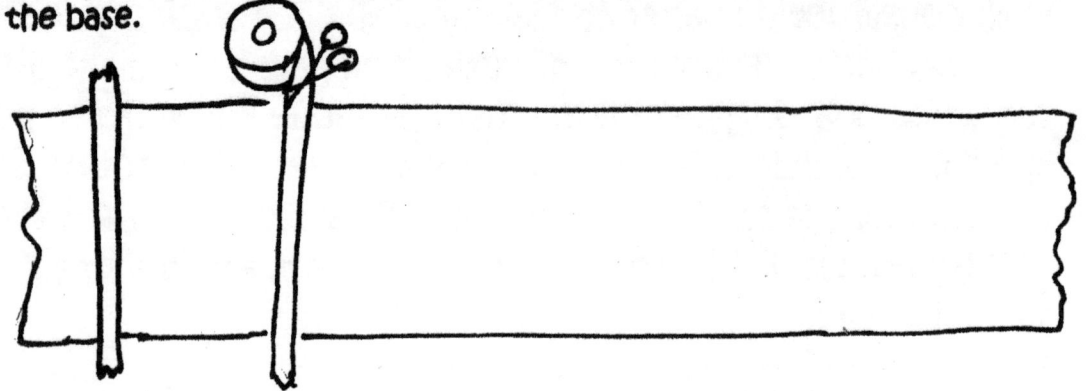

2. Use tape to make the boundaries for the top and the bottom of the boxes. The children place the sequence cards on the boxes when they do the activity. The boxes serve as a base for the sequence cards.

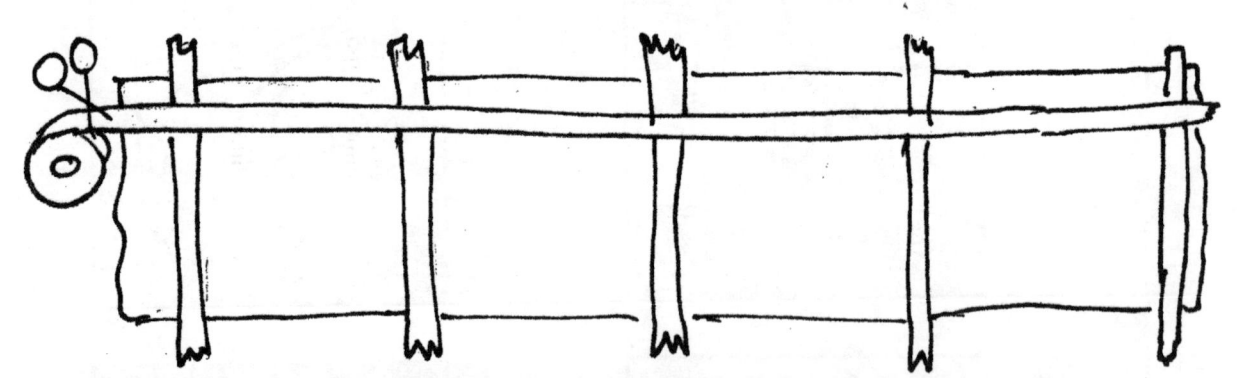

3. Trim along the outside edge of the tape while the garbage bag section is still taped to the table. Number the boxes "1" through "4."

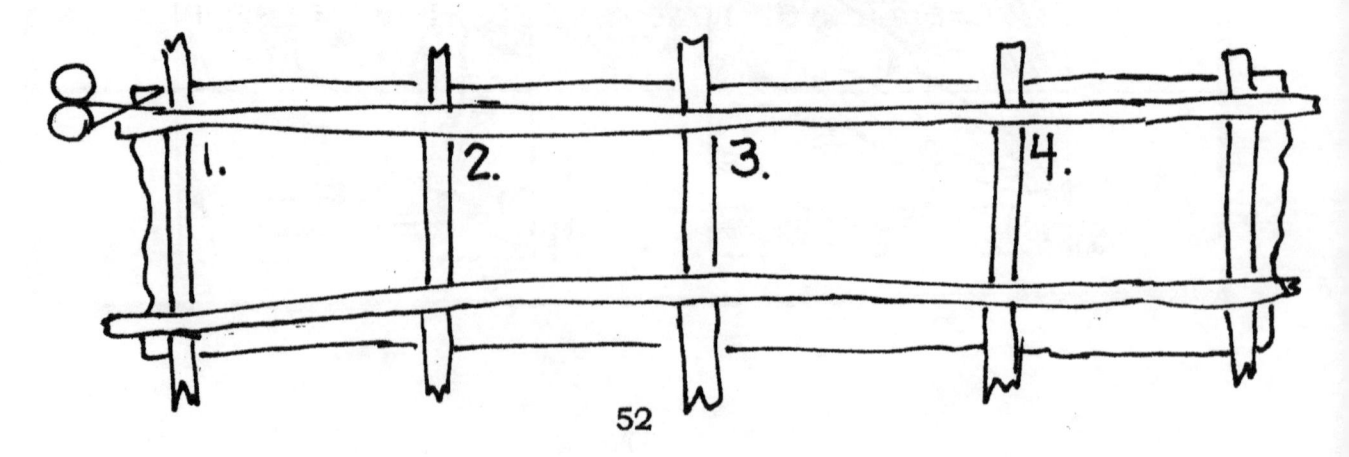

Frog Life Cycle Sequence Activity

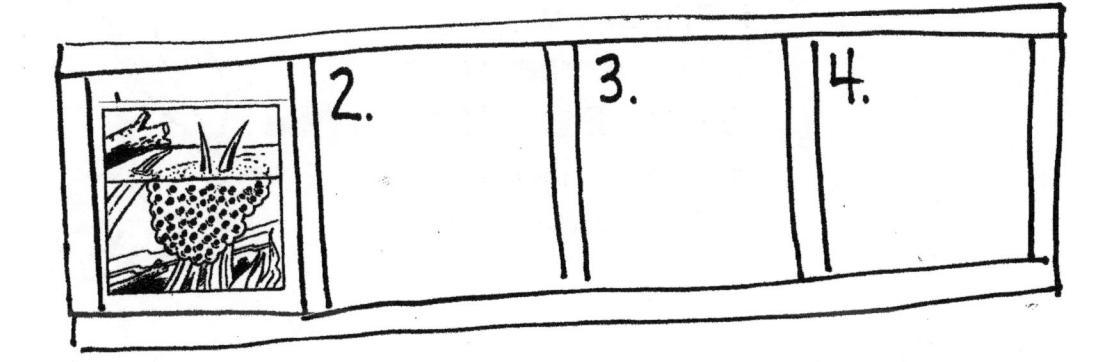

2. 3. 4.

Put the cards in the order that they occur. When you have finished fold up the base and store it with the sequence cards in the baggie.

12. Leaves
By Sharon MacDonald

Leaves are falling
One, Two, Three;
From the tree
Four, Five, Six;
Falling to the ground
Seven, Eight, Nine;
Ten leaves falling down,
Covering the ground.

Activities:

1. Sing this poem to the song *Are You Sleeping?*

2. Color the leaf patterns on page 55 and 56 in fall, or spring, colors. Number the leaves "1" through "10." Glue an 8-inch length of ribbon, or string, to each leaf stem. When you or the children read the poem, give each of 10 children one leaf; have them line up in order by the number on their leaf. Have them drop their leaves when they hear their number spoken.

3. Glue the numbers shown on page 57 to index cards, or short sentence-strips: One number per card. Laminate the cards. Glue a strip of magnetic tape to the back of each card. Write the poem words on a large poster board. In front of each number word in the poem, glue a magnetic-tape strip. Ask the children to match each number to the correct number-word (e.g., they would match "6" to "six").

Leaf Patterns

Leaf Patterns

4. For younger children, enlarge the leaf patterns on pages 55 and 56 to a size that would cover a child's hand. Color, laminate, and cut out the pattern. Write the numbers "1" through "10" on the leaves. Glue a strip of ribbon to the back of the leaf with a hot-glue gun. Have the child slip the leaf on his hand. The ribbon will hold the leaf in place. As you read the poem the children will hold up their leaf as their number is mentioned.

5. If you sing the poem, <u>hum</u> the number words and let the children sing them.

6. Change the numbers; count by "2s," by "5s," and by "10s."

7. Sing the poem in a round.

1 2 3 4 5

6 7 8 9 10

13. Ish Biddley Otten Dotten
By Sharon MacDonald

Ish Biddley Otten Dotten Bo Bo Ba Do
Ish Biddley Otten Dotten Bo Bo Ba Do
Ish Biddley Otten Dotten Bo Bo Ba Do
How are you?

Ish Biddley Otten Dotten Bo Bo Ba Do
Ish Biddley Otten Dotten Bo Bo Ba Do
Ish Biddley Otten Dotten Bo Bo Ba Do
Fine. Thank you!

Ish Biddley Otten Dotten Bo Bo Ba Do
Ish Biddley Otten Dotten Bo Bo Ba Do
Ish Biddley Otten Dotten Bo Bo Ba Do
Goodbye to you!

Activities:

1. Write the poem on a large sheet of paper; laminate it. Place a large sheet of laminating film over the song sheet; have the children find all of the "Bs" in the song by circling them on the overlay. Have them find other letters, too, like "O" and "D."

2. Have the children change the "Bo Bo Ba Do" to "De De Da Do" and "Ta Ta Ti Too."

3. Have the children use their imaginations to draw a "Bo Bo Ba Do" or an "Ish Biddley Otten Dotten."

14. Brown Round Tree
By Sharon MacDonald

There was little tree.
A little brown, round tree.
The brownest, roundest tree
I ever did see.
The tree was standing straight
With roots beneath the ground
And the wind blew the tree
To make the leaves fall down.

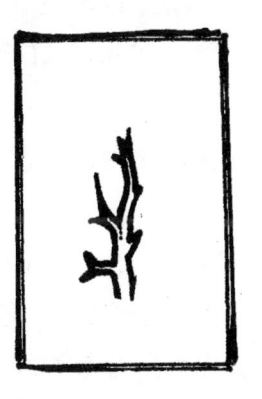

There was a little branch.
A little brown, round branch.
The brownest, roundest branch
I ever did see.
The branch was on the tree.
The tree was standing straight
With roots beneath the ground
And the wind blew the tree
To make the leaves fall down.

There was a little acorn.
A little brown, round acorn.
The brownest, roundest acorn
I ever did see.
The acorn was on the branch.
The branch was on the tree.
The tree was standing straight
With roots beneath the ground
And the wind blew the tree
To make the leaves fall down.

There was a little squirrel.
A little brown, round squirrel.
The brownest, roundest squirrel
I ever did see.
The squirrel was by the acorn.
The acorn was on the branch.
The branch was on the tree.
The tree was standing straight
With roots beneath the ground
And the wind blew the tree
To make the leaves fall down.

Activities:

1. This is an "add-on" poem. You can add new verses and new subjects. The children will love the variation: add-on an owl, a leaf, a bird, or an ant.

2. Make a continuous puzzle for the children. Write the key words "tree, branch, acorn and squirrel" on a sentence strip; leave a space next to the word large enough to glue a picture-- a tree, branch, acorn, squirrel--beside the word. Color and cut out the pictures for each key word; glue each one in place on the sentence strip. The pictures are next to the poem on page 59. Cut apart each picture-word pair using a unique scissor-cut pattern. For example, cut one section (tree with picture of tree) using a zigzag; the next, (the branch with the picture of the branch) in a curve; the next, in a block cut. Have the children put the puzzle together in the order that the words occur in the poem. (Please see directions on page 61.)

For more of a challenge, cut apart each picture-word pair. They will have to put the word and the picture together to solve the puzzle (please see the directions below).

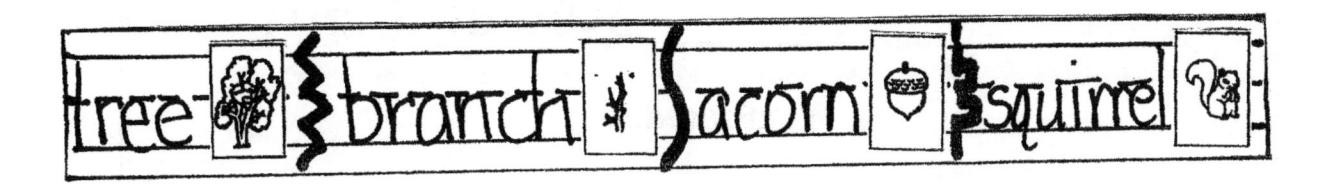

3. Make a tree book. Walk the children around the schoolyard to look at the trees. Get up close to a few of them. Ask them which one would they like to adopt? When you get back to the classroom, ask them to vote on a tree to adopt. (Please see pages 62-68 for the tree-book format; feel free to add other pages, as you like.)

Each day do a page of the tree book with all the children. In doing a tree-book project they will learn a lot about trees. Follow the outline on the next few pages to do your class tree book. Enlarge the half pages to full size to complete the book. This is a project that can be continued all year long.

Our Tree

By

_____ Boys and Girls

Dedicated to:

_____

Published by _____, _____, 2000

Cover

We voted which tree to adopt.

Tree 1_____	total votes _____
Tree 2_____	total votes _____
Tree 3_____	total votes _____
Tree 4_____	total votes _____
And the winner is! _____	

This is our tree. We named our tree _____.

(Photograph of the tree)

Page 1

Estimations and Predictions

We estimated that our tree was _____ feet tall.

We estimated that our tree was_____ years old.

We estimated that our tree has_____ branches.

We estimated that our tree has_____ leaves.

We predict that our tree will live_____ years.

We predict that our tree will grow to be _____feet tall.

Page 2

This is a leaf from our tree!

This is a leaf rubbing.

Page 3

Standard and Non-Standard Measurement

We used our bodies to measure the circumference of our tree.

```
┌─────────────────────────────────────────────────────┐
│                                                     │
│                                                     │
│                                                     │
│                                                     │
│ (Photograph of children reaching around the tree.)  │
└─────────────────────────────────────────────────────┘
```

It took _____ children to reach around it.

Page 4

We measured the circumference of the tree with a string.

```
┌─────────────────────────────────────────────────────────────┐
│                                                             │
│                                                             │
│                                                             │
│ (Photograph of the children using a string to measure around the tree.) │
└─────────────────────────────────────────────────────────────┘
```

We measured the string with a tape measure and it was ____ inches long. The circumference of our tree is _____ inches.

Here is our string!

(Staple a small, sandwich-size, resealable baggie here. Put the measuring string inside.)

Page 5

Using Our Senses to Gain Information About Our Environment

We *listened* to our tree with a stethoscope and we heard...

- _____
- _____

We used our ears to listen to our tree and we heard...

- _____
- _____

We learned that our senses can tell us what an object is *not!*

Page 6

Our Sense of Hearing!

(Photograph of listening to the tree with a stethoscope).

(Photograph of listening to the tree with their ears.)

Page 7

Using our sense of sight

We looked at our tree with...

- a telescope and we saw... _____
- a magnifying glass and we saw... _____
- a minifying glass and we saw... _____
- binoculars and we saw... _____
- our eyes and we saw... _____

Page 8

(Both boxes are for photographs of the children using different tools to examine the tree.)

Using tools to help us see our tree.

Page 9

Using Our Sense of Smell

```
(Photograph of children smelling the tree.)
```

We used our sense of smell to learn about our tree. It smelled like _____.

Page 10

Using Our Sense of Touch!

This is a bark trunk rubbing.

```
(Rubbing of trunk.)
```

We felt our tree with our hands and it felt _____

_____.

Page 11

Here we are making our bark rubbings!

(Photographs of children doing their bark rubbings.)

Page 12

Here is a picture of our tree!

Page 13

15. Cup Tapping
By Sharon MacDonald

These cups are made for tapping.
It's a funny little game I play.
I tap them here. I tap them there.
Come play my funny game this way.

Tap in and out and in and out.
Tap down and down and down.
Tap over, under, on your head.
Tap all your body 'round.

Activities:

1. Teach the children the poem. Next, have them tap along using paper or plastic cups, following the tapping instructions in the poem, shown on page 70. After they are comfortable with the movement patterns, let them make-up their own.

2. Make cup-tapping movement cards for the children; copy the cards on pages 71 and 72 several times. Color, back them with construction paper, cut out, and laminate them. As you can see on page 72, I have left one of the movement-pattern circles blank. Make up a cup-tapping movement pattern of your own and draw it in the blank circle (either you or the children can make one up). As you can see from page 73, put the cups, the tapping pattern cards, and the picture directions on a tray. The children can tap the cups along with the poem as you read it, or they can use the pattern cards to make new cup-tapping movements.

Cup Tapping

(Below are the cup-tapping patterns)

These cups are made for tapping

It's a funny little game I play.

I tap them here. I tap them there.

Come play my funny game this way.

Tap in and out, and in and out.

Tap down, and down, and down.

Tap over, under, on your head.

Tap all your body 'round.

Cup-Tapping Pattern Cards

Cup-Tapping Pattern Cards

72

Cup Tapping

1. Create a cup-tapping pattern with the cards.

2. Tap your cups to your pattern.

16. Names
By Sharon MacDonald

I have a name that's me, you see.
It is the name for me to be.
I like my name for it is me.
Can you guess what it could be?

It is not Sarah or Carlee.
It is not Harvey or Larry.
Is not Betty or Tyree.
Can you say my name for me?

Activities:

1. Have the children look for characteristics in each of their names as they work with the sentences below. Each week choose one of the sentences to write on a chart. The children hang with a clothespin on a clothesline, pin with a pushpin, stick with *Sticky Tac*, or hook with brads, the children's names that meet the requirements of the sentence. For examples, please see page 75.

If your name has the letter _____ in it, hang it here.
If your name begins with _____, pin it here.
If your name ends with _____, hook it here.
If your name sounds like _____, stick it here.
If your name has a CVC pattern, hang it here.
If your name has a CVCE pattern, stick it here.
If your name has a _____ blend, pin it here.
If your name has a _____ diphthong, stick it here.
If your name has a _____ diagraph, hook it here.

2. Other name-grouping activities are:

Find the children's names that rhyme.
Find names with two vowels, side-by-side.
Find names that have multiple letters in them (3, 4, 5, 6, etc.).
Put the names in the pocket chart in alphabetical order.
Place each name on the word wall next to the correct letter.
Find all the names with tall letters, hanging letters, rounded letters, and letters with dots.

If your name has the letter e in it,

hang it here.

Sue   George   Meg   Kiesha

17. How Do You Do?
Adapted by Sharon MacDonald

And we said, "How do you do?" to the lady bug!
And, "How do you do?" to the sheep.
And, "How do you do?" to the big kangaroo
Who is hopping around in his keep.

And we said, "How do you do?" to hummingbirds.
And, "How do you do?" to the bees.
And then to a pair of the scariest bears,
We said, "How do you if you please?"

And we said, "How do you do?" to the elephants.
They don't shake hands, they shake trunks.
While holding a rose at the end of our nose,
We said, "How do you do?" to the skunks.

And we said, "How do you do?" to the rattlesnakes.
We hollered "Hello" to the boa.
We all took a bow and we shouted out now-
We said, "How do you do?
How do you do?
How do you to the zoo!"

Activities:

1. Have the children say the names of the animals in the poem. Write them on a chart for the children to read again.

2. Encourage the children to build a zoo with blocks. If the children have difficulty doing this, post magazine pictures depicting zoo life or books showing animals in a zoo in the building area. Have plastic zoo animals available to use with the structure. Have index cards in a basket with pens

and pencils so the children can write the names of their animals on the cards. Have tape in the block building area so the children can tape their animal signs to the block areas they have built for each animal.

Note: if you cannot find plastic zoo animals, cut out pictures of zoo animals from magazines, glue them to stiff backing, and laminate them with clear contact paper or a laminating machine. Tape them to blocks so the children can move the animal-blocks around in the different areas.

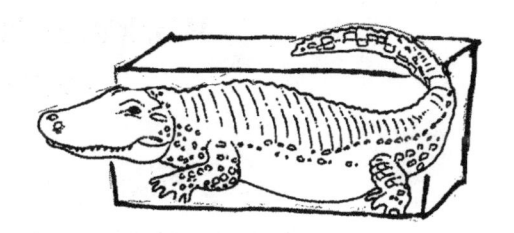

3. Collect plastic figures of the animals in the poem; write the animals' names on a sentence strip. Have the children match the figures to the names on the sentence strip. If you cannot find plastic animals, use pictures instead.

4. Write the words in the poem that are framed in quotation marks on sentence strips. Have the children match the words on the sentence strips to the words in quotation marks.

5. Have the children use highlight tape and cover all of the question marks in the poem. Afterward, have them highlight all of the "dos," all of the long- and short "O" words, and all of the words that are the names of the animals and insects.

18. Jump Down, Turn Around
Adapted by Sharon MacDonald

Jump down, turn around, and pick up the games.
Jump down, turn around, and put the games away.
Everybody's working to pick up the games.
Everybody's working to put the games away.

Work standing up! Work sitting down!
Work on your knees with the games all around!
Work standing up! Work sitting down!
Putting the games away.

Jump down, turn around, and pick up the blocks.
Jump down, turn around, and put the blocks away.
Everybody's working to pick up the blocks.
Everybody's working to put the blocks away.

Work standing up! Work sitting down!
Work on your knees with the blocks all around!
Work standing up! Work sitting down!
Putting the blocks away.

Jump down, turn around, and pick up the books.
Jump down, turn around, and put the books away.
Everybody's working to pick up the books.
Everybody's working to put the books away.

Work standing up! Work sitting down!
Work on your knees with the books all around!
Work standing up! Work sitting down!
Putting the books away.

Activities:

1. Use the poem at clean-up time. Choose the word that best describes what you are picking up: blocks, puzzles, toys, books, or games.

2. Write the poem on a chart. Replace the word "blocks," "games," or "books" with other words that describe what the children pick-up in the classroom. Give the children index cards with the names of the items written on them. Have each child pick a card and pick up that item. Then, the child can match the index card to the word on the chart and choose another card.

3. Write the letters of the alphabet on a large chart. Have the children find the words in the poem that begin with one of the letters; then, write the words on a chart next to the letters (please see the sample below).

A a	away	around	all
B b	blocks	books	
C c			
D d	down		
E e	everybody's		
F f			
G g	games		
H h			
I i			
J j	jump		

19. Pepperoni Pizza
By Sharon MacDonald

Make mine pepperoni,
Pizza, if you please.
Little sausage slices
In a pool of gooey cheese.

Make mine pepperoni,
Other pizza's fine.
You can eat all of yours,
And I'll eat all of mine

And I don't care about pizza crust,
I'll take it thick or thin.
No, I don't care about the pizza crust,
If pepperoni's in.

So...Make mine pepperoni,
Pizza, if you please.
Little sausage slices
In a pool of gooey cheese.

Make mine pepperoni,
Other pizza's fine.
You can eat all of yours
Please don't ask for mine.

Yes, make mine pepperoni,
Other pizza's fine.
You eat all of yours,
But, the pepperoniiiiiiiiiiiiiiiiiiiiii's <u>mine!</u>

Activities:

1. Copy the letters on page 81. Back them with card stock, laminate, and cutout the letters. Put them in a basket. Have the children spell the "Pepperoni."

p	e	p
p	e	r
o	n	i

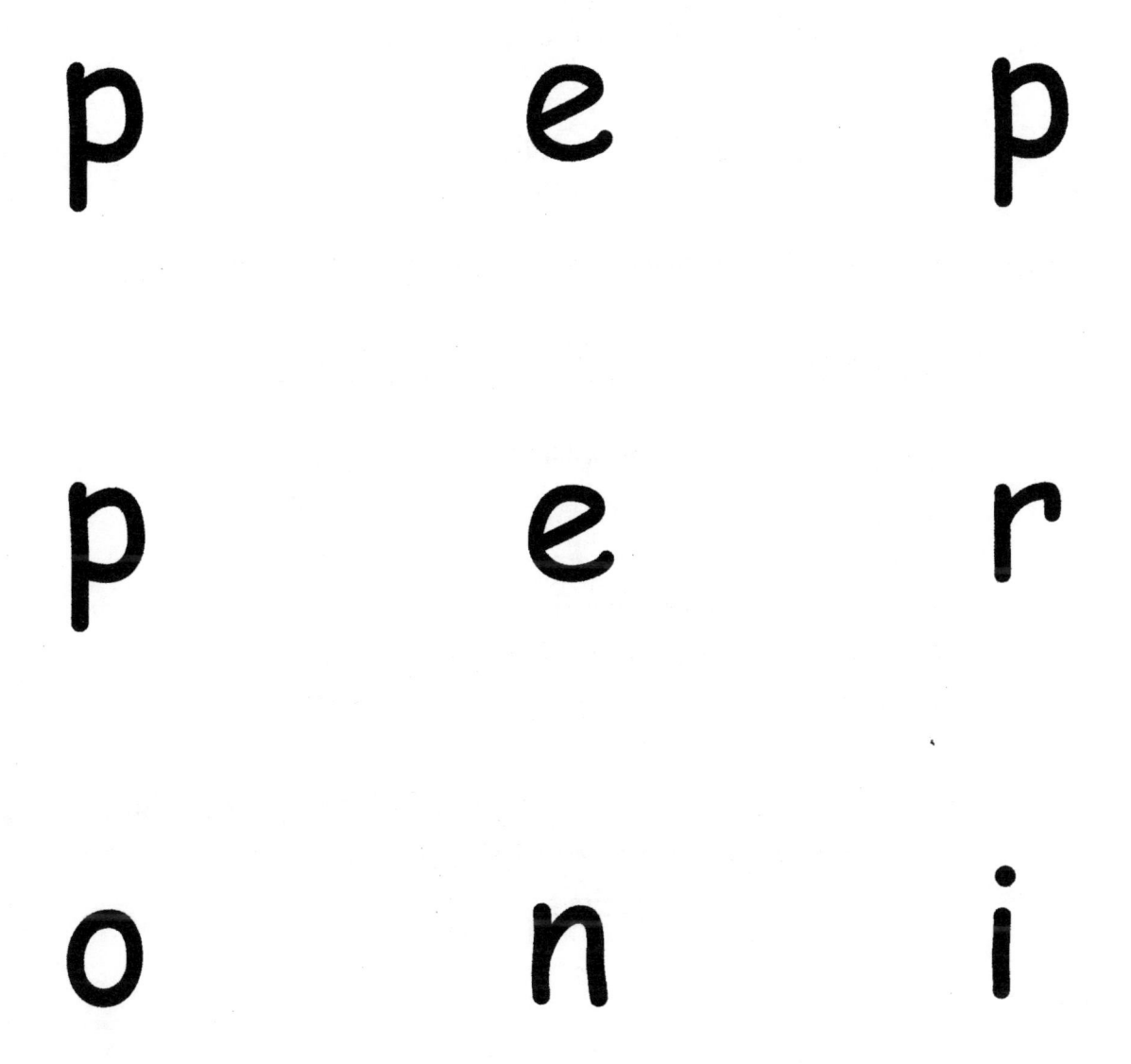

2. Copy the three menus shown on pages 82, 83 and 84. Collect "play" money for making change. Have the children figure the cost of the different kinds of pizza. Ask other children to pay for the pizzas. Use the "Activity" ideas on pages 85 and 86 with the "Menu" pages.

Mr. Gatti's Menu

Build Your Own Pizza

Start with our original, or pan-perfect crust, cheese, or one topping:

Delivered		Pick-Up
$6.99	~small~	$4.99
$7.99	~medium~	$5.99
$8.99	~large~	$6.99
$11.99	~two medium~	$9.99
$12.99	~medium & large~	$10.99
$13.99	~two large~	$11.99

Prices are plus tax; an additional topping is $1.25 per pizza. Limited delivery area. On time guarantee not valid for orders of 5 or more pizzas.

Toppings:

Provolone Cheese	Black Olives	Cheddar Cheese
Pepperoni Slices	Fresh Onions	Fresh Ground
Hamburger	Fresh Bell Peppers	Mild Sausage
Spicy Italian Sausage	Canadian Style Bacon	Jalapeno Peppers
Fresh Mushrooms	Anchovy Filets	Green Olives

Antonio's Pizza

(Our Pizzas are Available in Original, Hand Tossed Crust, Regular Thin, or Thick)

Toppings:

Meat:
Pepperoni   Salami
Beef   Bacon
Chicken   Anchovy
Canadian Bacon

Vegetables:
Mushrooms   Tomato
Black Olives Onion
Green Olives Jalepeno
Green Pepper

Cheese: Mozzarella Cheddar Parmesan

Cheese Pizza

7" X-small	10" small	12" medium	14" large	20" giant
$2.99	$5.99	$5.99	$7.99	$12.99

The Ultimate Pizza

10" small	12" medium	14" large	20" giant
$10.55	$13.99	$16.99	$25.99

Additional Toppings on:

7" X-small	10" small	12" medium	14" large	20" giant
c 45	c 60	c 90	$1.20	$1.70

Cici's Pizza

Take Home Cheese Pizza with One Topping

	small	medium	large	giant
	(10")	(12")	(14")	(16")
round	$2.99	$3.99	$4.99	$5.99
deep dish		$3.99	$5.99	

*All of our 100% real cheese is fresh shredded daily!
*All of our sauces and dough are made fresh daily!

Extra Toppings Only $.40 Each

~ Cheese ~ Pepperoni ~ Canadian Bacon ~ Ground Beef
~ Italian Sausage   ~ Mushrooms   ~ Green Peppers   ~ Onions
~ Green Olives   ~ Black Olives   ~ Pineapple   ~ Anchovies
~ Jalapeno Peppers

Super Deluxe (8 Toppings)   Large $7.79   Giant $8.79

Extras: Sauces to go $.25   Baked Pasta $1.99   Salad $1.99
Garlic Bread $1.99

$ Make $ Change $

1. If you bought a small, cheese pizza, and gave the cashier $3.00, how much change would you get back? (Antonio's Pizza Menu)

2. If you bought a medium, Pepperoni and cheese pizza, and gave the cashier $10.00, how much change would you get back? (Mr. Gatti's Menu)

3. If you bought a large, bacon-and-onion pizza, and gave the cashier $10.00, how much change would you get back? (CiCi's Pizza Menu)

4. If you bought a small, *Ultimate* pizza, and gave the cashier $11.00, how much change would you get back? (Antonio's Pizza Menu)

5. If you bought a small, and a large, cheese-pizza, and gave the cashier $20.00, how much change would you get back? (Mr. Gatti's Menu)

Buying Pizza

Refer to the questions below; use *Cici's Pizza* menu. Pay with play money.

1. How much money would you give the cashier if you bought a small, cheese-and-onion pizza?

2. How much money would you give the cashier if you bought a medium, cheese, onion, and pepperoni pizza?

3. How much money would you give the cashier if you bought a large, cheese-and-olive pizza and a salad?

4. How much money would you give the cashier if you bought a giant cheese-and mushroom pizza?

5. How much money would you give the cashier if you bought a small, and a large, cheese pizza?

6. How much money would you give the cashier if you bought a deep-dish, large pizza?

3. Have the children learn the American Sign Language hand-sign for "Pizza."

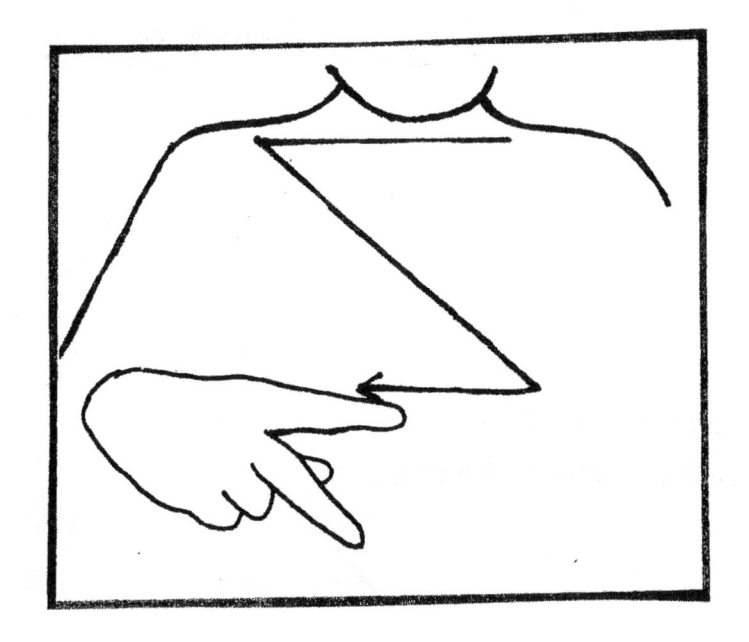

4. Get a small pizza circle; cover it with light-brown felt. Cut pieces from other colors of felt to make tomato sauce, pepperoni slices, olives, cheese, onions, mushrooms, and bell peppers (please see the pizza patterns on page 88). The children can put a pizza together and take it apart. Store the different pieces of the pizza in resealable baggies.

5. Have the children make their own pizza orders (use the forms on page 89). Have them make the pizzas to match the orders. Make multiple copies of the blank order form and have them available for the children to write pizza orders for other children.

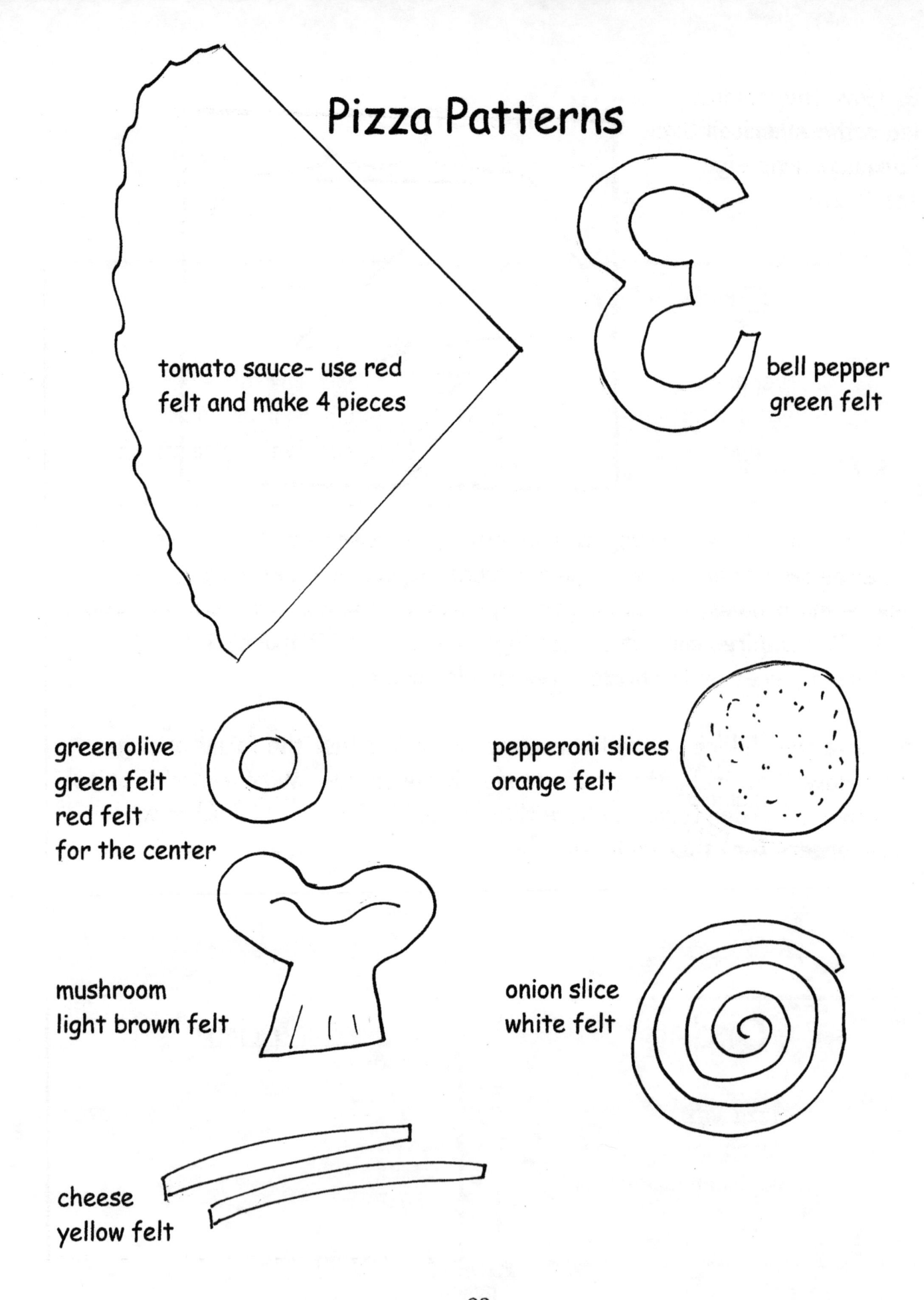

Pizza Patterns

tomato sauce- use red felt and make 4 pieces

bell pepper
green felt

green olive
green felt
red felt
for the center

pepperoni slices
orange felt

mushroom
light brown felt

onion slice
white felt

cheese
yellow felt

Fill the Orders

Order

1 pepperoni pizza with mushrooms and olives

Order

1 pizza with ½ olives, pepperoni, and onions; ¼ cheese and ¼ mushrooms

Order

1 pizza with ½ olives and cheese and ½ with mushrooms and bell peppers

Order

1 pizza with ¼ cheese, ¼ olives, ¼ onions, and ¼ pepperoni

Order

1 pizza with ½ bell peppers and onions and ½ pepperoni

Order

89